*"George Carey has written a pou...
on the marginalization of Christianity in Britain, arguing that
the law now militates against public expressions of religion,
especially if the religion concerned is the established church.
This is an important and disturbing book that should be read by
everyone concerned for the future of faith in Britain."*

– The Chief Rabbi, Lord Sacks

*"An important challenge to Christians to speak up for their
faith in public when they have opportunity. This reiterates the
warning given by our Lord against being ashamed of Him."*

**– Lord Mackay, Baron Mackay of Clashfern, former
Lord Chancellor (1987–1997)**

*"The Careys are not just celebrating 'Englishness' or
'Britishness', nor even the obvious importance of Christianity
for these islands. Their book is rather about the way in which
the Christian faith impacts on the day to day matters of life,
death, the family, justice and love. It is also an impassioned
plea for Christians to be allowed to bear witness to their faith
without fear of losing their jobs, their professional affiliation, or
their place in public life. It is an honour to be associated with
Lord Carey in some of his work in this area."*

**– The Rt Revd Michael Nazir-Ali, former Bishop of
Rochester and now Director of the Oxford Centre for
Training, Research, Advocacy and Dialogue**

"In this timely book, father and son have provided an invaluable resource for many Christians feeling threatened and confused in modern-day Britain. They discuss recent legislation and policies, shaped by the powerful influences of secularism, multi-culturalism and relativism, which have led to Christians being punished for expressing their faith and to many others feeling inhibited about speaking of their beliefs. They emphasize the need for Christians here to use our freedom to speak out in public – to affirm the rich contribution of our Judaeo-Christian heritage to our society, to challenge unfairness in any form, and to 'stick up vigorously and strongly for the Christian faith.'"

– Baroness Caroline Cox, Founder and Chief Executive Officer of the Humanitarian Aid Relief Trust (HART)

WE DON'T DO GOD

DO GOD

GEORGE CAREY
AND ANDREW CAREY

MONARCH
BOOKS
Oxford, UK, & Grand Rapids, Michigan, USA

First published in the UK in 2012 by Monarch Books
(a publishing imprint of Lion Hudson plc)
Wilkinson House, Jordan Hill Road, Oxford OX2 8DR, England
Tel: +44 (0)1865 302750 Fax: +44 (0)1865 302757
Email: monarch@lionhudson.com
www.lionhudson.com

ISBN 978 0 85721 030 2 (print)
ISBN 978 0 85721 273 3 (epub)
ISBN 978 0 85721 272 6 (Kindle)
ISBN 978 0 85721 274 0 (PDF)

Reprinted 2012.

Distributed by:
UK: Marston Book Services, PO Box 269, Abingdon, Oxon, OX14 4YN
USA: Kregel Publications, PO Box 2607, Grand Rapids, Michigan 49501

British Library Cataloguing Data
A catalogue record for this book is available from the British Library.

Printed and bound in Great Britain by Clays Ltd, St Ives plc.

In memory of Simon,
a beloved grandson and nephew.
1986–2010
*We thank you for the life and
love you gave.*

CONTENTS

CONTENTS

INTRODUCTION

There is a renewed and divisive debate in modern Britain about the role of faith in the public square. Only three weeks after its first publication, this book is being reprinted – a testimony to the public interest that this subject is generating. There are signs that the tide is turning in favour of openness and tolerance, values in which the British have long taken great pride.

Since publication, the case of Bideford town council hit the headlines yet again. The council's centuries-long practice of saying prayers at the beginning of meetings was held by Mr Justice Ouseley to be "incidental" to the functions of the council. He ruled therefore that Bideford had no power to commence its meetings with prayer. This turned out to be a pyrrhic victory for the National Secular Society, which had campaigned against council prayers on equality and human rights grounds. In fact, the judge dismissed their arguments, claiming that the degree of "embarrassment" felt by the complainant did not constitute an infringement of his freedom, any "more than is inherent in the exercise by others of their freedom to manifest their religious beliefs".

It was left to the Communities Minister, Eric Pickles, to point out that the Local Government Act of 1972, in which the powers of councils were strictly limited to prevent prayer, was about to be swept away by the government's Localism Act, leaving councils once more free to decide for themselves whether to have prayers, or not, at the beginning of their meetings.

This was followed, in February 2012, by a widely reported speech at the Vatican in which the Chairman of the Conservative Party, Lady Warsi, criticised a "militant secularism". In this powerful speech she said: "My concern is when secularization is pushed to an extreme, when it requires the complete removal of faith from the public sphere."[1]

Her concerns were echoed by a group of cross-party Parliamentarians who highlighted a "narrowing of the space for the articulation, expression and demonstration of Christian belief". The Christians in Parliament group examined some of the same court cases highlighted in this book and, like us, they concluded that a hierarchy of rights has been created. To break the impasse, they interestingly recommended the application of a legal test of "reasonable accommodation" to the rights of religious believers in order to gain them a proper and just hearing in the courts.[2]

Yet nothing has been resolved by these recent

---

1   "Britain being overtaken by 'militant secularists', says Baroness Warsi", *Daily Telegraph*, 13 February 2012.
2   "Christians not being persecuted in UK, report concludes", *Church Times*, 2 March 2012.

developments. There remains a deep malaise in modern Britain about the public expression of Christianity. At times it seems a "crusade" is being waged by the militant wing of secularism to eradicate religion in general – and Christianity in particular – from any role in public life. Yet this is only a small part of the story we tell during the course of this book. For the most part, the "unease" with which modernity regards the public manifestation of faith arises out of ignorance, historical forgetfulness, and well-meaning but mistaken "multiculturalism". There is a hard-fought conflict between a secular spirit and the Christian faith. We have no problem at all with an open spirit of enquiry or even unbelief. We believe wholeheartedly in the freedoms we have gained. To live in an open democracy where ideas flourish is something we have experienced in the West for centuries. The evidence from 2011's so-called "Arab Spring" is that this open democracy is something that is envied throughout the world.

In the course of this book we salute the few brave Christian souls who have had the courage to stand up against bullying tactics and, as a result, have lost employment. But what they have lost exactly is even more precious than jobs – they are the victims of injustice, for to hold to principles central to biblical Christianity is now being increasingly seen as unacceptable. We believe this to be wrong. Presciently, Tom Bingham, in his magisterial book *The Rule of Law*, states:

"You may believe what you like provided you keep your beliefs to yourself or share them with like-minded people, but when you put your beliefs into practice in a way that impinges on others, limits may be imposed, if prescribed by law, necessary in a democratic society..."[3] That is the crux of the matter. Tom Bingham, while acknowledging the fundamental role that the Christian faith has played in the development of the law, shows that the advancement of "human rights" has had the effect of removing a uniquely Christian belief system from the same.

This is the argument of our book. We are not pleading for special treatment for Christians, only for justice. It is our hope that the Christian faith that has blessed our nation more than most of us realize, may continue to flourish and make a positive contribution to our world. We believe that our current laws, and the way they are being implemented, are impeding the work of the church and challenging our effectiveness into the future.

I have no doubt that many will come to this book with different backgrounds and agendas; nevertheless it is squarely addressed to Christians and the churches. This book should be seen as a "call to arms", where our weapons are not weapons that hurt and destroy, but those that rely on truth, good will to all, and a deep faith in a Lord who calls us to follow him.

---

3   Tom Bingham, *The Rule of Law*, London: Penguin, 2011, p. 76.

It has been a great pleasure to write this book with Andrew, my son. I want to acknowledge the tremendous contribution – indeed, the lion's share – he has made. We are grateful to friends and family who have added to this book and who, in so doing, have strengthened its argument. Pride of place must go to our friend Barry Smith for his constant encouragement and, at times, gentle bullying. The Revd Dr Alistair MacDonald-Radcliff and Michael Poole, Visiting Research Fellow in Science and Religion at King's College London, have helpfully taken a look at various chapters, as have Andrea Williams and Paul Diamond. We are indebted to Tony Collins of Monarch Books for his patience, advice, and guidance.

CHAPTER ONE

LIVING IN CRITICAL TIMES

My decision to write this book was made on a precise date. It was 29 April 2010, when Lord Justice Laws' ruling in the case of Gary McFarlane (who had been dismissed from relationship counselling agency Relate because he refused to counsel a same-sex couple) declared: "We do not live in a society where all the people share uniform religious beliefs. The precepts of any one religion – any belief system – cannot by force of their religious origins, sound any louder in the general law than the precepts of any other. If they did, those out in the cold would be less than citizens, and our constitution would be on the way to a theocracy, which is of necessity autocratic."

As I read those words I realized how different my world view is from that of this learned judge and, at the same time, how ill-informed he was about the Christian tradition – and even less informed about the way that the Christian faith is woven into the history, culture, ethics, laws, and political life of the United Kingdom.

The curious thing is that in my witness statement (which Lord Justice Laws rejected) there was nothing that contradicted his words.

This witness statement arose out of my own sense of frustration on the part of some good Christian people, who had been dealt with harshly. I too am not arguing for a theocracy. Indeed, I am entirely at one with Lord Justice Laws in people having the same rights and being subject to the same laws. My objection to his ruling that led to the dismissal of a good man who had been a very good Relate counsellor for some years, is that it was now evident that if a person were a Christian and sought to live her or his life by Christian principles in the workplace, they would not get fair treatment. The interesting, yet very disturbing thing about Lord Justice Laws' presuppositions was that he assumed that the Christian faith had nothing to say about justice today and could be dismissed with remarks that bordered on the contemptuous.

As I read Justice Laws' summary I thought back to the Queen's Coronation in 1953 where the Queen was presented with a Bible: "To keep your Majesty ever mindful of the Law and the Gospel as the rule for the whole of life and government of Christian princes." Those powerful and precise words were not designed as a commitment binding on the young Queen alone; they were intended to signal that what our country stood for was a commitment to Christian values and teaching that stemmed from our foundational document. From 2 June 1953 to 30 April 2010, rather than the UK growing in greatness, we have witnessed a slow decline in moral values and a loss of memory regarding our indebtedness to Christian truth.

But it is all so puzzling. How is it possible that, in a country which has an established Church and a Queen who by tradition "defends the faith", that Christianity is being squeezed out or marginalized? Yet that very question dominates the pages of tabloid newspapers annually as they reveal yet more stories of nativity plays banned in schools; "Seasons Greetings" replacing "Happy Christmas" on the cards of political leaders; and the switching on of "Winter lights" rather than "Christmas lights" by twitchy local authorities. These may seem trivial examples, yet the same question was to dominate a BBC documentary by the well-known broadcaster, Nicky Campbell, in April 2010 under the title *Are Christians Being Persecuted?* While he concluded that persecution was too large a word for what was happening, he nevertheless pointed to a series of running skirmishes between Church and State, and the worrying signs of entrenched cultural warfare between the State's official religion, and the State itself.

We should avoid the word "persecution" because what

Christians face in Britain does not have that aspect of suffering for one's faith that many experience abroad – sadly, many in Muslim countries. Discrimination is a more accurate word, but for those who have lost their jobs because they have stood up for their Christian convictions it is entirely natural for them to feel that their experience is one of "persecution". The legal battles over the wearing of symbols of faith such as the cross by individual Christians, the sacking of staff because of their refusal to act against their Christian conscience, the cry of "foul" from some quarters when political leaders wear their faith on their sleeves can all be noted as examples of a society newly ill at ease with faith.

While these are well-known cases of secular ambivalence towards Christianity, behind them lies a new level of anxiety and alienation among believers. Church of England General Synod members have never been noted as unduly alarmist, yet a survey of them by the *Sunday Telegraph* in February 2009 found that up to two-thirds believe that Christians are discriminated against at work.[4] A further national opinion poll survey by the same newspaper in May 2009 revealed that this feeling was shared by Christians throughout Britain. One in five of respondents said they faced opposition at work because of their faith. More than half revealed they had suffered some form of "persecution" for being a Christian. Three quarters of those polled said they felt that there is less

2   http://www.telegraph.co.uk/news/religion/4622858/Christians-face-discrimination-in-workplace-say-church-leaders.html

religious freedom than twenty years ago. And a staggering 84 per cent of Christians thought that religious freedom of speech and action are now at risk in the UK.[5]

The truth on the ground is that Christians feel hemmed in as never before by often well-meaning legislation which they believe has had the unintended consequence of restricting religious liberties that have been taken for granted for centuries. In the light of recent cases in which public servants have been suspended for offering to say a prayer for members of the public, Christians question whether they can even mention their faith during their working life. The heavy-handed actions of some police in arresting street preachers makes them doubt whether they have the freedom to evangelize or share their faith. They ask whether they still have any freedom of speech, given the welter of hate crimes legislation during the past few years.

Can they any longer state traditional Christian views on the uniqueness of Christ without risking the charge of being prejudiced against those of other faiths? Is it possible to defend Christian marriage without being abused as "homophobic" and worse, arrested for inciting hatred?

The worrying aspect of these developments is that people who would in previous decades have been recognized as pillars of the community, now feel alienated and discriminated against. The rate of change has been bewildering and

---

3   http://www.telegraph.co.uk/news/religion/5413311/Christians-risk-rejection-and-discrimination-for-their-faith-a-study-claims.html

worrying for many ordinary Christians.

However, I do recognize that some Christians themselves scoff at the notion of "discrimination", or even a marginalization of Christianity. Some argue that it is high time that Christianity was divorced entirely from any supposed submissive role to the State, and its "privileged" status in the British constitution.

Christians who hold this view want a post-Christendom church, believing that Christianity sold itself out under Emperor Constantine in a Faustian pact with temporal power, which resulted in some 1,500 years of a spiritual dead-end. The uncoupling of Christianity from the machinery of State, the reduction of the Christian message to just another competing voice in a world of ideas of roughly equal validity, is simply a necessary evolution for the Church. It must be freed from the curse of privilege, prestige, and recognition to follow its true mission as Jesus Christ's community for outcasts, the poor, and dispossessed.

I understand the force of this argument and it may be that the time will come when the Church of England will, for the sake of its own dignity and independence, have to separate from an Establishment that is indifferent to the religious identity that once shaped it. But that time has not yet come because there are still very many people both within and without the Church who believe passionately that the Church in England (and in that I include all mainstream traditions) is still the backbone and sinew of what it is to be British. Indeed, this view is often echoed by those of other faiths who are just as disturbed as Christians by the erosion of faith in our land: secularism challenges all creeds.

This is an argument we will revisit later. However, it does not address the actual reality of the situation in which despite its established status, the Church has the freedom to pursue its mission. The novel situation that this book attempts to highlight is that under this new dispensation of a "neutral secularism", the first signs are that the mission of the Church is restricted. The brave new world into which secularists believe the Church may emerge with its integrity intact, may in contrast be a wholly bad thing. The signs point to restrictions in religious freedoms and an outcome that actually suppresses rather than releases the true voice of Christianity.

Can anyone still pretend that a secular State delivers neutrality? In fact, from the point at which it casts down state religion it makes a powerful statement of repudiation of the religious voice – all religious voices – in the public square. However, there appears to be no appetite for wholesale disestablishment on the part either of the public or of Parliament. As a consequence, the secularist strategy is simply to pretend that the current state of constitutional affairs does not exist. This has proved successful in spite of its dishonesty. Simply by pretending we live in a secular state, the secularist can make it so with a series of much smaller campaigning steps in that direction, such as seeking the abolition of the Lords Spiritual (the bishops in the House of Lords), or of faith schools. More audacious tactics include a national campaign to sue a West Country district council over the practice of saying prayers at the beginning of council meetings, completely sidestepping or ignoring the fact that prayers are said daily in the House of Commons, led by the Speaker's Chaplain.

The disappointing thing, of course, is that politicians have colluded in this dishonesty by neglecting the Church–State relationship progressively over recent Parliaments. From Prime Minister Gordon Brown's voluntary relinquishment of his part in appointing bishops, to the incomplete reform of the House of Lords, constitutional questions have been left hanging in the air to damaging effect on public confidence in our country's institutions. The former Bishop of Durham, N. T. Wright, currently Research Professor of New Testament at the University of St Andrews, has been one of the few voices raised in the House of Lords decrying constitutional reform "on the hoof" and calling for a Royal Commission to apply "joined-up" thinking to this state of affairs. His voice has been largely ignored.

The "new secularism" which will be observed during the course of this book has as its champion the atheist scientist Richard Dawkins whose challenges to faith have often been bad-tempered and ill-informed. His critique of faith reached its nadir with his claim that to bring up children in a faith is tantamount to child abuse. His is hardly an unrepresentative voice among the atheist community, though it has to be said that many atheists find his more outrageous statements embarrassing. Looking at the websites of national newspapers, whenever the question of faith is raised, one can see an astonishingly illiberal and intolerant attitude from atheists and secularists. There is an apparent fanaticism in this section of society, a fanaticism unrivalled in mainstream forms of British Christianity for decades, if not hundreds of years.

The task of this book then is to explore the roots of this distemper with the Christian faith and to present the argument that, far from enriching our nation when the Christian faith is stripped from our cultural and public life, our society will be infinitely poorer and far less united.

We live in critical times for Christian people. However oddly it might seem, I think the struggles that we face present an exciting opportunity to draw on the reserves of our faith, to present it once again to our nation as something that "makes all things new". Christianity began its life facing discrimination, which went on to become full-blown persecution. It has overcome many, many problems in the last two milliennia. It can triumph still.

CHAPTER TWO

WHAT HAS CHRISTIANITY DONE FOR US?

In our perennial debates on "Britishness" or "Englishness" that have flowed from Britain's identity complex as a nation, it has been intriguing to hear the powerful contributions coming from two immigrant bishops of the Church of England. Both bishops fled from real persecution in their homelands and have a profound sense of gratitude for the welcome they have been given in Britain. Yet both of them have given far more back. They are the Archbishop of York, John Sentamu, who as a High Court Judge in Uganda in the 1970s under the dictator Idi Amin was forced to flee to Britain, and the former Bishop of Rochester, Michael Nazir-Ali, who came to Britain from Pakistan in the 1980s when his family was threatened by Islamists.

In spite of their very different views on important matters, both men are playing a major role in reminding native-born British people of the remarkable legacy that is theirs. The Archbishop of York's call for the celebration of Englishness, and his reminder that our values are those of the Christian faith, has struck a chord with the British public. Similarly, Bishop Michael Nazir-Ali's prophetic blasts against multiculturalism – the doctrine that all cultures being equal, all must be treated the same – have gathered him a following outside regular churchgoers.

Both men have powerfully reminded us that a nation that forgets its past is likely to repeat tragic mistakes. In his resignation statement as Bishop of Rochester in 2009, Bishop Michael Nazir-Ali referred to a historical amnesia in British society, or at least a "selective sort of amnesia". He pointed to a forgetfulness about the Magna Carta, and widespread ignorance of Britain's role in the abolition of the slave trade, the age of universal suffrage, and the introduction of universal education – all of which were influenced directly and strongly by the Christian faith. However, he argued, our present focus on our corporate guilt over Britain's involvement in the slave trade, over its past complicity in forms of religious persecution, and over its involvement along with other European countries in exploitative colonialism has robbed Britain of pride in our achievements. Britons certainly need to repent, he agrees, "But repentance for past wrongs without the celebration of what has been good has deprived people of a common vision by which to live and a strong basis for the future."[6]

So at some point we have to ask ourselves: What has Christianity done for us? And like those revolutionary zealots in Monty Python's *Life of Brian* who posed the same question about the Roman invasion of the Holy Land, the answer is not immediately obvious. Yet once they started mentioning "sanitation, aqueducts and the roads", the answers in the *Life of Brian* kept spilling out. Surely, the same should be true of the contribution of Christianity to Britain?

An astonishing forgetfulness has gripped our public life. I became acutely aware of this during the 1990s when, during the preparations for the Millennium celebrations, there was a risible lack of clarity about the nature of the celebration itself. Both the Conservative and Labour Parties in the run-up to the year 2000 shared the same approach: "Yes, we want to celebrate the Millennium – but what is it actually about?" I remember recalling at the time that a massive cathedral building programme had coincided with the first Millennium of Christianity, bequeathing us buildings of grandeur and longevity throughout Europe. In the 1990s, government ministers and civil servants were planning a "Dome". This "Dome" had no coherent long-term purpose, no long-term future, and its contents were an after-thought. Virginia Bottomley, the Secretary of State for National

---

6 "Ignore our Christian values and the nation will drift apart", *Daily Telegraph*, 5 April 2009

Heritage in John Major's government, told me in the build-up to the Millennium that even some of the best minds in the civil service were ignorant of the Christian nature of the Millennium. For them and for others involved in the planning the event was simply the rolling of "9s" into "0s". The fact that the calendar itself began with "Anno Domini" ("The Year of Our Lord") apparently had little or no significance. No wonder that the Dome was so utterly forgettable that it is only making an impact on the public now that it has been turned into a venue for live events. It was not surprising then that negotiations with the government to establish a "Faith Zone" in the Dome were quite difficult, even though, under pressure, the Government agreed to the setting up of a Government/Faith committee on which I was represented through my chaplain, Colin Fletcher, whose effective contribution was rewarded with an OBE. And it was in this under-funded area – a poor relation to many of the other "Zones" – that the story of Britain's Christian heritage was told, particularly powerfully, through the lens of the Church's impact on our landscape. Photographs of church spires or towers in the distance on the landscape revealed how these graceful spires or rugged towers dominated rural Britain in a way that their forerunners, the scattered stones of prehistory, never did. A distant spire is a sign to the weary, hungry, thirsty traveller that a settlement is nearby with quite possibly a hostelry for food, drink, and board. The bells that ring out calling the faithful to prayer, or merely mark the passing of the hours of the day, have for centuries punctuated the lives of Britons. And this is only looking at the outward symbols and the buildings inspired by faith in Britain!

The untold story is the contribution – both good and sometimes bad – which the Church has made to the lives of people. An aspect of this is as a force for social cohesion. The church building has very often been the only venue in a town or village for gathering the community together. The contribution of churches to ordinary life has also come in the form of the occasional rites (baptisms, confirmations, weddings, funerals) by which the course of a human life has been marked out – from welcome to celebration to final farewells. Church festivals such as Christmas and Easter are still remembered through our Bank Holidays. Even now some of these festivals still have a profound influence on contemporary Britons, but in the past they were the occasions for communities coming together: family celebrations providing a break in hard-times and a blessing in the good.

Additionally, for centuries the Church has often been the sole provider of education to rich and poor alike. Hospitals, the roots of nursing, and more latterly the hospice movement have been inspired by the Christian faith. Many of our most significant charities had Christian foundations even if they have now downplayed the connection.

This is all to say nothing of the grand narrative of history:

our patron saints; the stories of the kings and queens and their connection with the Church; the Magna Carta – that manifesto of Christian freedom; and then the early modern revolution and reformation which saw the rise of parliamentary democracy founded clearly on Christian ideals of equality, and freedom. Even the beginnings of secularism are to be found in the Church's own political theology, with an easily recognizable separation of Church and State based on the sayings of Jesus in the Gospels and the writings of St Paul in the epistles, to be later developed into a highly influential vision of the "two cities" by St Augustine of Hippo. And in European history the influence of the Church on the great philosophers and scientists of the ages makes it implausible to repeat populist myths of a clash between religion and science. Up to this day, many significant scientists are still inspired by their Christian faith. Even our concepts of justice, from the Magna Carta to the growth of the common law, are founded upon Christian ideals, not least the Ten Commandments. The development of our ideas of justice and equality owes much also to Christian reformers. Pivotally, William Wilberforce (who campaigned on Christian grounds for the abolition of the slave trade) and other social reformers such as Lord Shaftesbury, heralded the beginnings of social reform in which all were at last counted as equal. The post-war achievements of a Welfare State and a National Health Service owe much to the contribution of Methodism and later Christian Socialism to the Labour movement, together with the campaigning support of that great wartime archbishop, William Temple.

Then there is the influence of the Bible and the Prayer Book on the English language. I doubt whether all that many people in Britain know the name of William Tyndale, but his contribution to the life and culture of Britons is incalculable. Tyndale's translation of the New Testament and parts of the Old Testament from Latin to English, first published in 1525, led to a major cataclysmic social change in Britain, though Tyndale himself was executed in 1536. Within a few decades, accessibility to the scriptures in the vernacular led to many becoming literate. The nonsense, often repeated, that Henry VIII created the Church of England completely sidelines the impact of Reformers like Tyndale, Cranmer, Latimer, and Ridley during the astonishing events of the sixteenth century. For decades before Tyndale's translation there was seething bitterness in Britain about the corruption of the medieval Catholic Church and a longing for reform. The Reformation arose from Europe-wide protests within the Roman Catholic Church that the crushing burden of ecclesiastical bureaucracy and the venality of the then Vatican was oppressing the poor and obscuring the Christian message. Martin Luther, an Augustinian friar, seized the moment to nail his 95 Theses to the doors of Wittenberg Castle and the Reformation took various national forms thereafter.

The shape that the Reformation took in England had the Bible at its heart and Tyndale's seminal contribution was quickly followed by other translations that culminated in the King James Bible of 1611. King James appointed a body of forty-seven academics to produce the Bible associated with his name, but in spite of the contributions they made, this version remains indisputably Tyndale's in that some 84 per cent of the New Testament and 75 per cent of the Old Testament is dependent on his translation. In 2011 we celebrated the 400th anniversary of this great translation, possibly the most influential book ever published in the English language. We can only hope in celebrating it, we shall have restored some public awareness of the genius of William Tyndale.

The influence of this version is acknowledged by some surprising critics of faith itself. Speaking in 2010, Richard Dawkins said of the King James Bible: "We come from a Christian culture and not to know the King James Bible is to be in some small way a barbarian." Then, perhaps, realizing that was in some contradiction to his avowed opposition to faith, he added, bizarrely: "It is important that religion should not be allowed to hijack this cultural resource." His caveat is scarcely surprising, considering that this Bible arose from people who believed with all their being that God had revealed himself in Jesus Christ. Melvyn Bragg, in *12 Books That Changed the World*, argues that "This bible (the KJV) has had more impact on the ideology of the last four centuries than any other creed, manifesto or dogma... [it is] a book of continuing universal influence" (Hodder & Stoughton, 2006). This influence has shaped the greatest minds in the English language: from Shakespeare, on to Milton, Bunyan, Wesley, Newman, Darwin, Wordsworth, Dickens and T. S. Eliot. Dickens once said, in a letter he wrote to the Revd D. Macrae: "All my strongest illustrations are drawn from the New Testament: all my social abuses are shown as departures from its spirit. In every one of my books there is an express text preached on, and the text is taken from the lips of Christ." The influence of the English translation of the Bible is nearly matched by that of the Book of Common Prayer on the life of the English people and its contribution to our nation's literacy. This too was first published in the sixteenth century. When I was Archbishop of Canterbury one of the most memorable and moving daily reminders of this powerful history came in the Lambeth Palace chapel. I was just a few yards away from the very place where Thomas Cranmer, archbishop during the reign of Henry VIII, wrote the 1549 Prayer Book that is so central to liturgies of the Church of England today. A revised version, published in 1662, is still in widespread use. Without exaggeration we can say that for hundreds of years, the Prayer Book was the partner of the Bible and central to the life of the nation. If we owe the Bible to Tyndale, it is to the genius of Thomas

Cranmer that we are indebted for the Prayer Book. Indeed, each book was a companion of the other as literacy spread throughout the nation and throughout the English-speaking world. The cadences of Cranmer's Prayer Book and the eloquent and rolling beauty of the King James Version have inspired and blessed the English people.

The Reformation that gave rise to the restoration of the Bible at the heart of the Christian faith in Britain was responsible also for another legacy, namely our progress as a free nation and, eventually, as the first industrialized country. Unshackled from the power of an authoritarian Church, the legacy of the Reformation was to have a role in liberating the individual conscience and enabling unfettered scientific research and exploration. It is certainly true that in Britain it took several centuries to pass before other forms of Christianity were given the same rights as the Church of England, but this does not affect in any respect what the Reformation did for Britain. Although there were many other factors behind the industrialization of Europe and America, it is no accident that this took hold first in Protestant societies.

Some claim that the most important influence on modern Britain was never Christianity itself, but the Enlightenment. The name "enlightenment" (*Aufklärung*) is given to that period of European history in the eighteenth century where, throughout Europe and in the new nation known as the

United States, a general intellectual and social movement began to challenge the dominance of religious authority. Independent thinking and the flourishing of individualism were fundamental to this widespread upsurge of knowledge. Central to it was a questioning of traditional authorities, morals, and customs. Strictly speaking, it is not possible to disentangle the various strands of this rich and somewhat chaotic movement of the human spirit, but two stand out. One led to the liberal democracies of the West, and the other to the French Revolution and the overthrow of authorities that were thought to quench the freedom of the masses. The consequent Reign of Terror launched by Robespierre, Danton, and others shame the name of Enlightenment. In Britain and America the first strand regarding the liberal democracies of the West and which are associated with John Locke, Alexander Pope, Isaac Newton, Thomas Paine, Thomas Jefferson, and Benjamin Franklin is arguably more important.

It is claimed today that in order for social and intellectual progress to be established, the power of the Church had to be confronted and its hegemony challenged and destroyed. A myth has grown up that the powerful thinkers I have mentioned above challenged the Church's role as the appointed interpreter of God's will and the Bible's authority over moral matters. However, this is a distortion of history. Such thinkers as Locke, Pope, and Newton never saw themselves as challenging the authority of the

Anglican Church to which they had great loyalty. Indeed, Locke uttered that he was a "Church of England man". The regrettable "theism" that Jefferson and Franklin espoused and which even many Anglican clergy and some archbishops of Canterbury, such as Tillotson embraced, belonged more to the tenor of the times – until the nation was awakened by the Evangelical Revival of the Wesley brothers. The Wesleyan movement has often been credited with Britain's turning aside from the French path of revolution.

The sidelining of the Christian faith in Britain has seen its European counterpart in the many voices wanting to marginalize Europe's Christian heritage. No one with any sense of history can ignore the huge impact that the Christian faith has made on Europe (and, indeed, on both South and North America). However, there are those in mainland Europe who contend that, in spite of Christianity's contribution to the past, what matters now is not forms of faith or outdated morals, but a future built on techno-scientific achievements. A thinker who has led the attack against such ideas is Pope Benedict XVI whose trenchant views need to be heeded. The Pope argues that disregard of the rich legacy of Christian thought, art, literature, and law leads towards a moral and intellectual desert. "What is European culture," he asks "and what has remained of it? Is European culture perhaps nothing more than the technology and trade civilization that has marched triumphantly across the planet? Or is it instead a post-European culture born on the ruins of the ancient European cultures?" The Pope's conclusion, echoing the historian Arnold Toynbee, recognizes the crisis of the Western world, which he attributes to the abandonment of religion for the cult of technology, nationalism, and militarism. For Toynbee this crisis had a name: secularism.

However, there is a much simpler way to trace Europe's indebtedness to the Christian faith, and that is to follow the advice of the Polish historian, Krzysztof Pomian, presently Scientific Director of the Museum of Europe in Brussels. Pomian suggests the most positive way to understand a civilization is to study it from outside and, in the case of Europe, to ask "How different is it from, say, Chinese civilization?" He replies that what unites Europeans is a unique visual and aural landscape. He draws attention to features such as the presence of crosses on buildings and in cemeteries and sometimes at crossroads and roadsides. Then there is our measurement of time. Sunday, an official holiday, begins each week. The European year is similarly punctuated with feast days and holidays. Certain feasts, in particular Christmas and Easter, are common to western and to eastern Europe, although celebrated on different dates because the religious calendars do not coincide. Holidays are specific to each country, but each has a national holiday or a Victory Day. Then, again, Europe possesses its own cultural references. If we try to establish which titles, names, events, and places are referred to with the greatest frequency in European writings, the visual arts, religious and civil ceremonies, political discourse and so on, we arrive at the conclusion that, apart from those disseminated by Christianity on all continents, almost all are either ignored outside Europe or known only to small and learned minorities. Another dimension, Pomian notes, is the status of women. Europe only recognizes monogamous marriages; women are not required to cover their faces and they have played an essential role in the continent's culture and politics. A significant element he notes is the absence of dietary restrictions, another legacy of Christianity and quite different from Judaism and Islam.

This convincing survey of the elements that show the centrality of Christianity in European life forces us to ask: Why do some wish to deny the power of this influence and to downgrade the role of religion? The answer can only be found in a conscious desire to find a common identity for Europe not in religion, and certainly not in its founding religion, but in secularism itself. Religion, it is deemed, is so unreliable, divisive, and shaky a platform for unity that it is necessary for it to be replaced with a bland "nothingness" that makes no demands and calls for no commitments. The unintended consequences of this are to be found in our present confusion and lack of moral compass. Indeed, the decline of a moral conscience grounded in absolute values is the legacy of the Enlightenment. Left untreated, it could lead to the self-destruction of the European conscience and Europe's moral vision.

So where does that leave us today as a nation still in debt to our Christian heritage and living off that rich heritage? We are left with a puzzle. The symbols of a rich faith continue to exist in many different ways in our nation: prayers in every parliamentary day; the establishment of the Church of England; the role of churches in civic life; and the chaplaincies in hospitals, prisons, and the armed services. Relatively recent legislation still insists on a mainly Christian education in schools' religious education, with assemblies in schools of a Christian character. Despite a rapid rate of immigration and a much greater plurality of faiths in modern society, the vast majority of Britons still count themselves as Christians. In the 2001 Census, 72 per cent claimed to be Christian. And the rise in popularity and success of faith schools is a testament to their success academically as well as a signal that many parents still believe that a Christian ethos provides a moral compass for their children.

Yet there are other statistics that point ominously in a different direction. Church attendance has declined sharply in the past century. While fifty years ago over half the population of the UK would go to church on a weekly basis, today only about 15 per cent attend church on a monthly basis. We cannot deny that our nation, along with most of western

Europe, is drifting towards an unthinking secularism.

However, there are reasons for encouragement. Even the most pessimistic doomsayers have been proved wrong about the "death of God" and the secularization of society. In fact, faith is resurgent in the world today with religions throughout the world showing growth in the developing nations, offsetting the decline in western Europe. Even in Europe there are signs that although attendance at church is sporadic and infrequent for many people, there remains a significant proportion of the population – much greater than those who attend football games, for example – for whom the church remains a part of their life. Even the Church of England has a success story to tell of rising numbers of worshippers in big cities such as London, of rising rolls at Easter and Christmas services, and of bigger congregations in flagship churches, such as cathedrals. Furthermore, among the newer evangelical and Pentecostal churches many new congregations are being established and Christian festivals such as Soul Survivor are attracting tens of thousands of young people every year. The story is not all of demise and decline.

CHAPTER THREE

THE CHANGING STATE OF BRITAIN

The theme of the iconic 1979 hit, "Video Killed the Radio Star", by The Buggles is that of "nostalgia" in a fast changing world. The song tells the story of a 1960s singer whose career is cut short by the advent of television. The powerful image of a heart broken by "pictures" is repeated in the final verse of the song. And the blame is firmly put on the influence of VTR. It must be remembered that even when the song was recorded by The Buggles, the technological revolution of video tape recorders (now almost totally obsolete) was only at its beginnings. Computer technology was in its infancy dominated by devices like the ZX81 and later the clunky Amstrads. How many of us then could have imagined iPads and netbooks except in Science Fiction fantasies? Many households had only just progressed from black and white televisions to the coloured variety. High definition was not even a twinkle in the inventors' eye. Video technology in the home was split between the contesting claims of Betamax and VHS. Pity those who for a few years veered down the dead-end road of Betamax, though even this technology was superseded a few years later by DVDs which seem to have already had their day. Mobile phones were vast things, the size and weight of a housebrick. Compare these now to smartphones, which grow increasingly sophisticated by the day.

The point is that enduring popular songs even in that period were concerned with the exciting and alarming advances in technology which had the power to create fame and consign "stars" to the dustbin of history at a switch of the button. Even in 1979 before the revolution was fully underway we mourned the passing of an age in which everything was simpler. We looked back with longing to a time when there was less choice. These dilemmas are by no means new. Thomas Hardy's novel *Under the Greenwood Tree* features a similar battle between technologies – in Hardy's case he laments the fact that church orchestras were superseded by the pipe organ. In recent years things have come full circle as traditionalists decry the churches now that strip out their pipes in favour of a music group.

In other words, there was never, ever a "golden age" in the past to which we can look back as a solution to the travails and concerns of the present. The problems of the past were often different but were equally real. Christians, like others, always need reminding that though the past may seem an appealing place, we can only deal with the hand we are given.

RAPID SOCIAL CHANGE

Nevertheless we live in a period of particularly rapid change. Even more far-reaching and fundamental than the development of new games platforms, the rapid advances in digital technology, and the ubiquity of computers have been the new ways of relating together which these advances have brought about. Social networking, texting, emails, blogs, Twitter, and Facebook have introduced new ways of interacting. Have you noticed that it is far easier to be offended by what you read online than by a face-to-face conversation? Even if you are engaged in a robust argument in your everyday life it is rare that you will be truly offended. In real life, you can read body language and walk away if necessary. Eye contact is a vital way of communicating, whereas in the online world everything is so instantaneous and so direct that experienced users of virtual reality have long invented terms such as "trolling" and "flaming" to describe the sheer levels of rudeness, and vitriol, that you can encounter. Such ways of interacting online are in danger of infecting our everyday discourse. Examples of "mob rule" on Twitter are enough to give anyone cause to wonder about the kind of society we might become.

These new ways of relating have been accompanied by rapid social mobility, and enormous social fragmentation. We no longer meet together in all-age neighbourhoods, communities, and villages in a geographical way as we used to. The churches have caught up with this fact, with some success, by establishing churches along cultural lines. "Fresh Expressions" are initiatives by which new churches, seeking to relate to peer groups such as skateboarders, surfers, parents, and children, are given official blessing.

In some senses, we are then a more balkanized and divided society than ever before, even in comparison to times where whole communities were isolated by distance. We are now drawn to each other by interests, work, and age groups, rather than gathering as families of all ages in geographical proximity.

Another significant change in this period of innovation, mobility, and fragmentation, has been the breakdown of traditional models of family. Marriage is no longer the preferred choice for young people seeking serious relationships: indeed, marriage is chosen by less than half of such couples. "Partner" has now superseded "husband" and "wife" as the preferred title. Single motherhood across generations has become a norm in some disadvantaged communities. Serial monogamy is also a new pattern of relationship. Children are often brought up in step-families or by a single parent and many of them, according to a mass of research, are disadvantaged by family breakdown, and through the lack of a father figure. It is clear that people still desire marriage and stability for their children yet no longer have the tools or increasingly the role models to work on their relationships during the toughest times.

Only a short while ago marriage was actually recognized and valued in the tax system. The Married Person's Allowance was watered down in the 1980s and 1990s until its abolition became irresistible. And later when the leader of the Conservative Party, David Cameron suggested recognizing marriage again by a tax allowance much of the reaction was one of bemusement. How could "marriage" be rewarded by the State in preference to alternative family relationships? This reaction ignored the fact that marriage, according to a growing body of research, remains the best and most stable way of bringing up children who then go on to have the best chances in life. Indeed, as marriage is devalued, in spite of direct evidence of its importance in sustaining the quality of family life, the social cost of alternative relationships is a growing burden on the State and on local authorities.

PLURALISM AND THE FAMILY

This new attitude towards pluralism in family life coincided with perhaps the most rapid cultural movement in history – the establishment of homosexuality as a social and sexual norm. On the one hand, it could be said that from the decriminalization of homosexuality in 1967 it took nearly four decades before the first civil partnership gave homosexual relationships the same legitimacy in law as heterosexual ones. In reality the greatest strides to equality were taken when the Labour government came to power in 1997. Within a very short time, the controversial Section 28 of the 1988 Local Government Act which barred the promotion of homosexuality in schools was abolished and the age of consent equalized. And in 2004 the very first civil partnership was blessed. Together with these changes a whole raft of equality measures were put in place to give homosexual orientation particular protection.

During this period public attitudes to homosexuality changed rapidly. Whereas in 1983, 62 per cent thought homosexual acts were "always" or "mostly wrong" this had changed to 36 per cent in 2008. The British Social Attitudes Survey revealed that some 39 per cent didn't think homosexual acts were wrong at all. Similar changes had taken place in the course of these same twenty-five years in attitudes to cohabitation and divorce leaving the population substantially divided on issues of sexual morality for the first time in history.

LEGISLATIVE INCONTINENCE

One other major change that has taken place in recent years is the surge in legislative activity on the part of Parliament. In 2007 the law firm Sweet and Maxwell released to the press their research into the rate of legislative change under three prime ministers. They found that an average of 2,663 new laws were added every year under Tony Blair, compared to 1,724 under Margaret Thatcher. Yet this is not an issue that is confined merely to Labour governments. The greatest increase in legislative activity was under John Major, introducing 39 per cent more laws per year than Thatcher, while Blair enacted 11 per cent more laws than Major.

At the very least the statistics demonstrate a long-term trend for successive governments to legislate more aggressively especially in areas such as criminal law, where forty Criminal Justice Acts were introduced in the first ten years of Blair's premiership.

Much of this new legislation was reactive in responding to the perceived concerns of society and the media. Len Sealy, a Cambridge law professor, was quoted in the Sweet and Maxwell findings, pointing to a blame/compensation culture that demanded something was done about every accident or event. "Whether this is an issue of health and safety, consumer protection, discrimination, putting a regulation on the books or increasing a penalty makes a political point."[7]

The leader of the Liberal Democrats, Nick Clegg, has referred to this renewal of the parliamentary workload as "legislative diarrhoea". Nevertheless these new laws coincide with a large amount of EU legislation that automatically becomes law without passing through the Houses of Parliament. Furthermore the Sweet and Maxwell research finds that an added phenomenon was not simply the number of statutes but their size. Many of them run into hundreds of pages. The Companies Act of 2006 set parliamentary history weighing in at over 700 pages with 1,300 sections.

In order to get through the workload, Parliament routinely deals with new legislation as "statutory instruments" meaning that there is less debating time and less scrutiny.

The question that must be asked is how many of these laws lie uselessly on the statute book never to see the light of day once they have passed. They cannot possibly all be needed including the much talked about law against nuclear explosions. This legislative incontinence has led to two major problems. Firstly, it leaves the vast majority of people in a position of uncertainty. They don't know where they stand within the law. People today are much more likely to be committing an offence unknowingly. Furthermore, we

---

7   http://www.sweetandmaxwell.co.uk/about-us/press-releases/260607.pdf

are entitled to ask whether so many of these laws have been properly thought through and scrutinized before they enter the statute book.

LEFT BEHIND

I marvel when I see my grandchildren having the world opened to them by the use of computers. At the touch of a key they have the resources of a library before them on the computer screen. I can only marvel at the advantages they have when they do their homework. Yet what about those who are left behind? How do technologically impoverished children fare in education nowadays?

With every "advance" there are always those who are deserted and left in a state of bewilderment and distress. This is just as true in the area of social attitudes as it is in ICT. With this shift of thinking about marriage and sexuality has come a whole raft of laws to enforce the new norms. The equality laws designed to protect human rights have been extended to give sexual orientation the status of a "protected characteristic" alongside race and gender. While it is a far from settled question whether sexual orientation is an immutable characteristic or not, nevertheless we must behave and talk as though it is.

This new orthodoxy on sexual behaviour brooks no

opposition. In 2003 the Bishop of Chester was publicly admonished by the Chief Constable of Cheshire Constabulary after he had told a local newspaper that some homosexuals may be able to reorientate themselves with specialist help. A complaint was made to the police who announced an investigation. While there were clearly no grounds for prosecution nevertheless the Chief Constable, Peter Fahy, released a statement in which he criticized the bishop and said, "All public leaders in Cheshire need to give clear leadership on the issue of diversity."

In 2005 the family values campaigner, Lynette Burrows, was called and "lectured" by the police after appearing on a BBC radio programme which discussed gay adoptions. She simply said on the programme that adoption by a homosexual couple was not in the best interests of a child prompting a complaint to the police from a listener.

The Northern Irish MP Iris Robinson was also investigated by police in 2008 for expressing her religious beliefs about homosexuality on a BBC Radio Ulster debate.

It is not only prominent people whose views are reported in the media who are challenged in this way when they dare to differ from orthodoxy but many ordinary people as well, including a number of street preachers. Chillingly, an elderly couple were subjected to eighty minutes of questioning by police officers after "politely" complaining to their local council about its gay rights policy. Joe and Helen Roberts of Fleetwood in Lancashire were visited by police who were told by the council that they had made a "homophobic telephone call". The police told the couple they might have committed a "hate crime". After a later legal challenge both council and police admitted they were wrong to treat the Roberts in such a way.

In January 2006 leaders of the Gay Police Association called for members of the Christian Police Association to be barred from the Metropolitan Police because of their views on sexual ethics. And in the same year a group of Glaswegian firemen were disciplined by the Fire Service for refusing to march in a "gay pride" rally. One of the firemen, John Mitchell, later successfully overturned the disciplinary decision after the Strathclyde Fire Board admitted they had failed to take account of his religious beliefs.

TURNING BACK THE CLOCK

Just as the clock cannot be turned back on technological change, so it is with social change. The genie is out of the bottle as far as new sexual rights and the plurality of different kinds of "families" are concerned. Christians should not dream nostalgically of a less complicated age, but engage with the present. However, it remains true that many Christians find themselves in the position of more than a third of the population in continuing to think that homosexual acts are wrong. If the rights of religious believers are to be respected some accommodation must be sought by the authorities with these very deeply held views. Furthermore, the right of Christians to express these views in a courteous manner with respect for the views of others must continue to be tolerated.

TRUE TOLERATION

The very word "toleration" is an important one; it is a word that has fallen out of fashion in recent years. To "tolerate" is often seen as a somewhat begrudging response to cultural and moral differences. Instead of "tolerance" of different lifestyles and beliefs, with which we may disagree, we are now told that we must accept these differences as all being equally valid.

It has to be said at this point that even as I make a plea for greater tolerance, I am aware of the regrettable and shameful history of the ostracism, persecution, and punishment of homosexuals and those who campaigned on their behalf. The alliance of the law and the public teaching of the Church have had some very oppressive outcomes especially in the days before the decriminalization of homosexuality. Yet we must also remind ourselves that it was only in 2008 that the blasphemy offences were swept away. These laws were used to torture and punish atheists and Nonconformists among others, and had a negative effect on the kind of tolerance and free speech that I am advocating.

Yet many Christians until very recently opposed both the decriminalization of homosexuality and the abolition of blasphemy as an offence. So if we are to argue for the freedom of Christian expression, and the public manifestation of our beliefs in the public square, we must acknowledge this history and repent. Furthermore, we should not seek special rights, or denigrate the freedom of others. When the Religious Hatred Act 2006 was being debated in the House of Lords I, and many other peers, successfully opposed draconian "wording" which we believed would have a chilling effect on freedom of speech. The campaign outside Parliament featured the comedian Rowan Atkinson, famous for his portrayals of weak-kneed clergy, who rightly argued passionately that limits should not be set on the freedom of comics to make jokes even at the expense of religious believers who, it has to be said, often take themselves far too seriously.

CHRISTIAN FREEDOM

This chapter could have been called "Stop the world, I want to get off", for very many Christians and others are in the position of being utterly bewildered and distressed by developments which they themselves cannot understand or agree to. To take the example of changes of language in another area of equality, there are large numbers of people in Britain today for whom politically correct language about other races is a mystery. They are still using what were once regarded as polite terms such as "coloured" to refer to "black" people without realizing that usage has changed. I suggest that the last thing these "left behind" members of the public need is the weight of the Equality and Human Rights Commission thrown at them.

The same goes for all those so-called social "Luddites", such as traditional Christians, who lag "behind" the new orthodoxy on homosexual rights. If those championing far-reaching social changes are so convinced that theirs is the side of progress then they can afford to extend a little understanding. Alternatively, they might consider that just as Christians must find ways of coming to terms with a new plural landscape, they also have to accept the expression of a diversity of views, even those which differ from the prevailing norms.

CHAPTER FOUR

THE ATTACK ON CHRISTIANITY

In the wake of the massive social change we observed in the previous chapter, two other major factors have conspired to put further pressure on Christianity: secularism and multiculturalism. Though a residual attachment to Christianity continued to inspire the British public it cannot be denied that the institution of the Church is now weaker than it ever has been. As an optimist, I have always pointed to statistics that tell the tales of success such as the growth of worship in cathedrals, the success of mission in cities like London, and the persuasive merits of initiatives such as Alpha. Nevertheless, the decline in the number of churchgoers over successive decades of the twentieth century cannot be disguised by these glimpses of hope.

Inevitably, other ideas have inexorably increased their reach steadily into the vacuum replacing Christian mores, norms, and tradition. Almost unnoticed these ideas have had a drip-drip effect and now modern Britain has reached a point where it is almost completely changed. The growth of secularism has been one of the most prominent movements of change. Edward Norman, in his book *Secularisation*, observes that it is extraordinary how individual Christians are so unaware of just how secular their own lives have become under the new social order. "The English Church has to operate in a situation of deep and deepening, secularity. Expressed in its greatest simplicity, this means that daily life is largely bereft of reference to religion," he writes.[8]

At the heart of this for Norman is the fact that while Christianity survives in some form constitutionally, politicians now shy away from any reference to religion. This attitude permeates society down to the family in which parental discipline is based not on Christian belief but on an appeal to self-interest. "There is now no higher note at the centre of the life either of society or the state," he soberly reminds us.[9]

This has, of course, taken place in many practical and unseen ways. There is the increasing tendency of public leaders not "to do God", together with selective amnesia about the fact that we have an established Church so cannot be considered in any meaningful sense to be a completely secularized society. Yet the vestiges of Christian consciousness are now quietly neglected. For example, many state schools now

---

8   Edward Norman, *Secularisation*, London: Continuum, 2002, p. 42.
9   Ibid.

ignore the legal requirement for a daily act of Christian worship. Other schools are now moving to a standardized spring break because the date of Easter varies from year-to-year. The neglect of the traditional Easter holidays is yet another sign of the increased dislocation between society and faith.

Another aspect of this dislocation has been the weakening of religious programming by the BBC. Although *Songs of Praise* has recently celebrated its fiftieth anniversary, the fact is that according to a 2009 report to the Church of England General Synod, religious coverage has fallen by about 15 per cent in the last twenty years in a period when its total television output has doubled.[10]

"These things have happened," remarks Peter Hitchens, "not because of the rage against religion in Britain... but because the British establishment has ceased to be Christian and has inherited a society with Christian forms and traditions."[11]

When all that is left of the Christian establishment remains in the hands of a largely secularized government, widespread confusion can be the only result. Our political classes are left asking the question: What do we do about the inconvenient vestiges of Christianity?

---

10 "Church of England to confront BBC over treatment of Christianity", *Sunday Telegraph*, 20 June 2009.
11 *The Rage Against God*, Continuum, 2010, p. 90.

MILITANT SECULARISM

It is hardly a surprise that when the Christian faith is so little understood so much ignorance about it should arise. For the most part, the militant secularism popularized by "New Atheists" such as Richard Dawkins and Christopher Hitchens is based almost entirely on a straw man version of the Christian faith. Norman again writes: "Christianity is now often represented, in television and journalism, and in the classroom, as the author of many wrong attitudes... It is regarded, often with very insubstantial historical backing, as tainted with racism, sexism... as the agent of slavery, of persecution and of a large catalogue of evils... inhibiting social progress."[12]

Yet, I am not entirely unsympathetic to aggressive secularism. There is bad religion around – in all religions. Christians should be concerned when their faith, rooted in the example and teaching of Jesus Christ, is associated with fundamentalism of the very worst kind, intolerance, and bigotry. On a spectrum of belief with former right-wing American leader of the "Moral Majority", Jerry Falwell, at one end and Richard Dawkins at the other, I would probably have greater sympathy with Richard Dawkins.

There are aspects of evangelicalism, particularly American evangelicalism, that downplay intelligent discourse and civilized debate. I must emphasize that this tendency is in

12 Norman, p. 45.

the minority but because it exists, and because it feeds the widespread media fancy that much evangelical thinking is located with the fairies, it lends credence to the idea that Dawkins and Hitchens must be right. But they are profoundly wrong. There is more good religion than bad and there is a strong rational element to faith that transcends the atheistic fundamentalism peddled by such writers.

Those who champion secular humanism are now campaigning against church schools. They complain about the provision of chaplaincies in hospitals, prisons, and the armed forces. They seek to remove state funding from Christian charities or erect hurdles of compliance which would make it impossible for Christian charities to apply for funds without abandoning their objectives.

One of the more egregious examples of an aggressive secularism has been exhibited in the continuing dispute over council prayers in the Devon town of Bideford. A member of the council objected to the tradition of beginning meetings with a prayer by clergy from the town. Despite being voted down in successive meetings this councillor decided to challenge the democratic decision in the courts with national funding from secularist groups. His claim was that the council's practice of public prayer was discriminatory against those of other faiths and atheists. Picking upon a small district council which could ill afford to defend the case seems a particularly cowardly way of seeking to outlaw public prayer completely. The National Secular Society cannot have forgotten that Parliamentary proceedings open every day with prayer in both Houses.

The Roman Catholic composer James MacMillan, conductor of the BBC Philharmonic Orchestra, urged religious leaders to resist "increasingly aggressive attempts to still their voices". In his lecture to the Sandford St Martin Trust in 2008, he pointed to a survey showing that only a fifth of those working in television describe themselves as religious compared with seven in ten members of the public. "If this is the case with the TV industry, you can be sure it is the same for the metropolitan arts, cultural and media elites."

In a 2006 interview in the *Daily Mail*, the Archbishop of York, John Sentamu, argued that the BBC default view is that Britain is "secular and atheist". He added "We are fair game because they can get away with it."[13]

And despite the fact that the militant tendency of secularism grew in strength in the wake of the September 11 attacks, the particular target is Christianity, rather than Islam. This is primarily because "Christianity" remains in some ways the faith that belongs even to most secularists. It is also poses the most significant obstacle to their goal of a completely secularized Britain.

---

13 "Archbishop blames 'chattering classes' for collapse of Britain's spiritual life", *Daily Mail,* 13 November 2006.

MULTICULTURALISM

Multiculturalism is not, in itself obviously hostile to Christianity. Nevertheless this modern doctrine has had far-reaching consequences for Christianity in modern Britain. The multiculturalist approach to immigration, for example, replaced attempts to integrate or assimilate immigrants. It held that cultural diversity was a positive good for Britain and that each culture should be recognized and respected.

This relativist approach refused to give any faith or culture any pre-eminence over another. Of course, the multicultural option is self-contradictory because it puts our society in the position of tacitly approving restrictive cultural attitudes to women, despite overtly valuing the equal role of women in the modern world. The most obvious problem with multiculturalism, which has now largely led to it falling out of favour, was the fact that rather than bringing unity in diversity it led to separate communities which rarely, if ever, touched upon each other. Against the backdrop of extremism in the Muslim community, Trevor Phillips, previously one of the main proponents of multiculturalism, called in *The Times* in April 2004 for its abandonment. "What we should be talking about is how we reach an integrated society, one in which people are equal under the law, where there are some common values."[14]

Just as secularism can hardly be held to be a neutral

14 "Britain must scrap multiculturalism", *The Times*, 3 April 2004.

value system, so multiculturalism did great damage to the Church in Britain. If all faiths were held to be equal then even the faith which was by law established and reflected the tradition of the majority of Britons could not be emphasized and celebrated any more than any other. This had the most obvious consequences in terms of now annual tabloid stories of local councils and officials getting overly sensitive about the public celebration of Christmas in their anxiety not to offend other faith groups. Consequently we had the shortlived but well-known spectacle of Birmingham Council rebranding Christmas in 1998 as "Winterval" in order to include other religious traditions in the celebrations. Such bureaucratic nonsense became commonplace with councils bending over to represent Diwali and Eid in their festive lights. Companies and corporations sent out cards with "Seasons Greetings" rather than "Happy Christmas" while it became increasingly hard to find any representation of the Baby Jesus, Shepherds, or Wise Men on the shelves of greetings cards shops.

One of my favourite examples is that of the college which removed Christmas and Easter from the staff calendar to avoid offending ethnic minorities. From henceforth employees were told they should refer to Easter and Christmas holidays as "End of Term Breaks" to "increase inclusion and diversity". Then there was the bizarre event in which the Tayside police rushed to apologize to the bemused

Muslim community for including an image of a puppy on its advertisements after being told that dogs were regarded as unclean animals by Muslims. A Muslim spokesperson was reported to have said, "There isn't any Islamic basis for taking issue with a simple picture of a little puppy."

In fact, that was the problem with this whole politically correct phenomenon. Faith groups were patronized by this approach as though they were over-sensitive children offended by even the mention of another belief. As Archbishop of Canterbury I became friends with the prominent leaders of many other faiths. They laughed at such widespread attempts to protect their sensitivities. In fact, they valued public manifestations of Christianity as Britain's established faith and were not offended by celebrations of Christmas and Easter in the least. They cherished the Christmas cards they received from their Christian friends and wanted to be included as far as possible in Christian celebrations. Just as it is a privilege for a Christian to be invited to celebrate Passover with a Jewish family, or Eid with a Muslim one, even if we cannot always share each other's beliefs, this feeling is usually reciprocated. In fact, I would go further and say that for the most part the leaders of other faiths welcomed even the establishment of the Church of England, because it afforded them a greater hospitality than secularism could ever offer. Secularism drives faith voices out of the public sphere, whereas the establishment of Christianity guarantees the public role of faith.

THE FINAL DESTINATION

So what is to be the final destination of our society? An inexorable drift to total secularism or relativism? There is nothing to suggest that either state of affairs is inevitable.

If Christianity is finished, why are opponents so obsessed by it? Terry Eagleton, a Marxist and atheist, is a thinker who is deeply interested in faith and has an accurate understanding of theology. He remarked in a *New Statesman* article "Societies become truly secular not when they dispense with religion but when they are no longer agitated by it."[15] This is far from the case. Indeed, one could argue that even in non-churchgoing Britain, faith still occupies a place in the centre ground. There is no one remotely interested in attacking flat earth views, because the idea is dead. I am struck by the fact that secular magazines, such as the *New Statesman,* examine religion on a regular basis. Christianity still fascinates. It is as if the opponents of faith cannot quite believe their own argument.

Millions of people in Britain believe that faith in God is a powerful force for good and that the churches make enormous contributions to the common good in this land

15 *New Statesman*, 22 June 2011.

and throughout the world. Roy Hattersley, former Deputy Leader of the Labour Party and himself an atheist, wrote: "Good works, John Wesley insisted, are no guarantee of a place in heaven. But they are most likely to be performed by people who believe that heaven exists."[16]

We Christians have been weak in our defence of the Christian faith in the face of such forms of secularism. This is curious when one contemplates the result of this ideology over the last forty or so years. Where is the evidence that, at a time when it is claimed that Christianity has failed, that secularism ushers in a better life for others? All the evidence points the other way: more crime, broken families, acceptance of cohabitation instead of marriage, soaring numbers of teenage pregnancies, and a general decline in moral values and standards. A report in an Australian paper stated that a madam of a large brothel in Sydney has complained to the local council about plans to build a church nearby, saying that it will attract the wrong sort of people to the area. What I am arguing is that this form of secularism, which drives faith from the heart of a nation, undermines the very moral values that make it work. It is difficult to resist T. S. Eliot's conclusion that "A people without religion will, in the end, find that it has nothing to live for."

---

16 "Faith does breed charity", *Guardian,* 12 September 2005.

CHAPTER FIVE

FAITH IN THE PUBLIC SQUARE

In 1979, Margaret Thatcher, Britain's first female prime minister, stood on the threshold of No 10 Downing Street, quoting an ancient yet famous Christian prayer by St Francis of Assisi. She memorably said: "Where there is discord, may we bring harmony. Where there is error, may we bring truth. Where there is doubt, may we bring faith. And where there is despair, may we bring hope."

There was no great controversy over her choice of a Christian prayer to mark her triumphal entry into the history books. In fact, although Britons were easily embarrassed by conspicuous displays of religiosity, they were nevertheless at ease with religious imagery, and commonly known prayers. It would be rare to find a Briton who didn't know the words of at least one prayer, usually the Lord's Prayer. And there was still an easy familiarity with the Christian story. Yet this was not the 1950s; churchgoing was in a state of lamentable decline, and the climate for faith was beginning to get colder. And while a greater proportion of the population still chose the Church of England to baptize, marry, and bury them than they do today, nevertheless in the 1970s there was a much greater relaxedness about faith. It was an important aspect of British life, and the Church as an institution was still central.

Less than a quarter of a century later, a fiercely atheist press secretary to a Downing Street successor was insisting, "We don't do God." Alistair Campbell's famous 2003 utterance was made to cut short a question by *Vanity Fair*'s David Margolick to Campbell's boss, Tony Blair. To be fair to Alistair Campbell's interruption, he did at a later stage add that he had no intention to deny the place of faith in public life. He interrupted, he said, because "My 'We don't do God' was simply part of a view that in UK politics, it is always quite dangerous to mix religion and politics." Nevertheless, his intervention is widely held to represent a shift in the relationship between faith and politics.

It is worth noting that before each became prime minister, both Tony Blair and Gordon Brown were comfortable in both talking about their faith, and writing about how they were both inspired by Christian thinkers and Christian theology. In fact, they were both inheritors of a very strong Christian socialist tradition within the Labour Party which dated from the middle of the nineteenth century and included figures such as Denison Maurice, Charles Kingsley, and Thomas Hughes.

Tony Blair's reticence about his Christian faith only lasted until his resignation as prime minister. Within months he had converted from Anglicanism to Roman Catholicism, the faith of his wife and children, as well as forming the Faith Foundation to aid interreligious dialogue and action on development and poverty.

Tony Blair later admitted to a BBC One programme on *The Blair Years* that he didn't talk about his religious views while in office for fear of being labelled "a nutter". He said that unlike American voters who were at ease with the expression of religious views, their British counterparts would imagine their leaders communing "with the man upstairs and then come back and say 'Right, I've been told the answer and that's it.'"

This distrust in public attitudes towards faith seems to characterize much thinking today. Jeremy Vine, the BBC Radio 2 presenter, revealed in 2009 that he would find it impossible to talk about his faith on his radio shows. He added that there was something "socially unacceptable" about revealing that you believed in God: "You can't express views that were common currency thirty or forty years ago. Arguably, the parameters of what you might call 'right thinking' are probably closing."

The idea that religious belief is "nutty", or socially unacceptable seems to be deep-seated at least in the circles in which Jeremy Vine and Tony Blair move. Whether this is true in wider society is much more open to question. Religious belief after all remains commonplace in Britain today. Despite being told by secularists and atheists that God was dead, religious belief and practice has been remarkably persistent. This is true globally but it is also true in Britain and other Western societies. In recent years the numbers of religious believers have been added to by mass immigration. And it is not just religions such as Sikhism, Islam, and Hinduism that have benefited from a flood of exiles: eastern Europeans have flocked to Roman Catholic churches – a fact which prompted headlines in 2006 that for the first time the number of regular Roman Catholic worshippers had overtaken Anglican worshippers. The Church of England is growing in large cities like London, while cathedrals report significant rises in attendance, especially during the major festivals of Christmas and Easter. In 2001, when the national census revealed a staggering 72 per cent still calling themselves Christian, there was no sense on the part of these people that by ticking a box they were signalling that they had the equivalent of an embarrassing social disease.

Notwithstanding this underlying religiosity I have found that in the Westminster bubble very many politicians, civil servants, and political advisors are either completely secularized or assume that fairness and true objectivity demand a "secularist" approach. They make occasional positive noises about faith schools, primarily based on those schools' successful results. They dare not bring their reforming secularist zeal to the constitution and the establishment of the Church of England partly out of a respect for our highly popular Queen. Furthermore constitutional reform doesn't win you any votes and it takes an extraordinary amount of parliamentary time and energy. Yet they behave as though the Church of England was already disestablished, and very often appear to believe that church schools are a success in spite of their faith commitment rather than because of them. They are by no means hostile to faith, merely ignorant of it.

It is this ignorance that is behind so many statements we hear by politicians and others in the media that we live in a "secular democracy". Hazel Blears was especially fond of using this phrase when she was Labour's Communities Secretary. She once said: "We live in a secular democracy. That's a precious thing. We don't live in a theocracy, but we've always accepted that hundreds of thousands of people are motivated by faith. We live in a secular democracy but we want to recognize the role of faith."[17]

Hazel Blears, for whom I have a great deal of respect as a politician, should have known better that the alternative is not "secular" or "theocracy". In a nation which has an

17 "Hazel Blears says sidelining of Christianity is 'common sense'", *Daily Telegraph*, 9 June 2008.

established Church in both England and Scotland, our form of democracy steers a steady course between these extremes. Faith is central to our constitution in the Coronation Oath and the establishment of the Church of England yet we have never been a theocracy and never will be. That such a prominent government minister should so blithely ignore Britain's constitutional arrangements in which the monarchy, Church, and Parliament are so closely interrelated speaks volumes. I referred earlier to the difficulty the Church of England faced in the 1990s to persuade Whitehall and Westminster that the Millennium was more than a matter of the "9s" rolling over into "0s". Hazel Blear's insistence falls into a similar category of such amnesia. Illustrative of the point also is the long campaign by the Roman Catholic Church for a reference to Europe's Christian heritage in the proposed European Constitution. This campaign was ultimately a failure, though the Constitution was rejected in any case in a referendum by the French in 2005.

In 2008, such widespread ignorance was laid bare in an important report on the Church of England's contribution to social welfare provision by the Von Hugel Institute . The report's authors pointed to a "significant lack of understanding of, or interest in, the Church's potential contribution in the public sphere". The sheer range of activity by churches and charities was far below the radar of evidence gathering by the Charity commission and departments of state.

The "Moral, But No Compass" report[18] found that the government had underestimated the number of faith-based charities by as much as 50 per cent. Clergy and church workers complained about a "profound religious illiteracy" on the part of central government and local authorities.

EXEMPTIONS

Another way in which there has been a gradual marginalizing of faith in the public realm is much less noticeable because it is more about omission than it is about commission. In 1967, for example, it was absolutely natural when the Abortion Act came into being to allow exemptions for doctors who on the basis of ethical or religious convictions were opposed to abortion. Similar protections were given to shop workers and others when the Sunday Trading laws were changed. Even in 1998, when the government incorporated the European Convention on Human Rights into British law, the Church lobbied hard for its own exemptions on employment, which the government eventually granted. In recent years, however, the government has been unsympathetic to such persuasion. The passage of the Sexual Orientation Regulations was dogged by difficulty. These regulations prohibited any discrimination in the provision of public

18 Francis Davis, Elizabeth Paulhus and Andrew Bradstock, Von Hügel Institute, St Edmund's College, Cambridge, Matthew James Publishing, 9 June 2008.

goods and services. On the face of it, they were a thoroughly good thing, but Church leaders began to wonder whether the government had realized that these regulations would make it impossible for Roman Catholic Adoption Agencies to any longer discriminate in favour of married couples. In fact, the government had realized, but there could be no compromise, and no exemptions despite the fact that Roman Catholic agencies often placed more difficult children with couples.

Leading secularists are now urging the government to take away the limited exemptions which the Church already has in the area of employment. Dr Evan Harris, a leading member of the Liberal Democrats, called on the government to abolish exemptions for religious charities contributing to the so-called "Big Society".

Although he conceded that it was "unjustified to argue against religious organizations providing public services, as it is discriminatory to single out those with a religious ethos", he pointed to the "extra challenges" faith groups posed. His claim was that the exemptions given in UK law in regulations and the Equality Act are too wide because they allow religious organizations to discriminate in a limited number of leadership jobs. He believed that such exemptions enabled faith groups to impose a religious test on both its employees and the users of the services which the Church supplied.

He suggested bizarrely that this amounted to "religious

persecution" about which he warned the Liberal Democrats were not prepared to sit back and do nothing.

Dr Evan Harris' intervention is a chilling reminder that what the State has given by way of exemptions to enable such groups to remain faithful to their faith can just as easily be taken away again. The churches are absolutely dependent upon the limited tolerance of a largely religiously illiterate and disinterested state.

TOTALITARIANISM

It must be asked at some point whether this supposed forgetfulness about Britain's, or indeed Europe's, Christian past and present is accidental or deliberate. There are increasing signs of very real opposition to Christianity itself across Europe. In 2004, the Italian president nominated Rocco Buttiglione as Justice Commissioner of the European Union. A storm of criticism met the announcement and eventually forced the withdrawal of his nomination. The controversy focused on his conservative Catholic views on homosexuality, marriage, and the upbringing of children. *The Times* writer, Matthew Parris, usually a moderate voice, wrote in October 2004: "I say enough of tolerance. I do not tolerate religious superstition, not when it refuses to tolerate me. Sweep it from the corridors of power."[19]

19 "Sweep out religious superstition which will not tolerate me", *The Times*, 23 October 2004.

Buttiglione himself told a hearing of the European Parliament's Committee on Civil Liberties, Justice and Home Affairs, that his personal opinions would not prevent him dutifully administering his office. He was qualified enough for the job since he speaks a number of languages and had served as Minister of Europe in Berlusconi's government, yet his Christian beliefs were unacceptable. In the *Christian Science Monitor* in 2005 he later bitterly reflected on his experience: "The new soft totalitarianism that is advancing on the left wants to have a state religion. It is an atheist, Nihilistic religion – but it is a religion that is obligatory for all."[20]

And before anyone says that it could only happen in Europe and not in Britain, the former Home Secretary Ruth Kelly met a similar reaction when her membership of the conservative Roman Catholic group, Opus Dei, was revealed in the media. Additionally, there was a storm from gay rights groups and secularists when Joel Edwards, the former Evangelical Alliance leader, was appointed to the Equality Commission.

More recently, a Christian GP was sacked after only a month on the troubled Advisory Council on the Misuse of Drugs. Complaints about Dr Hans-Christian Raabe were not concerned with his undoubted expertise on drugs nor his ability to advise the government, but actually over the

---

20 "What place for God in Europe?", *Christian Science Monitor*, February 22 2005.

infelicity of not "disclosing" a paper he had written which linked homosexuality to child sex offences.

The Christian commentator and medical expert Peter Saunders said about the case that the references Dr Raabe made to homosexuality and paedophilia were merely quoting Home Office papers. "In bowing to political pressure on this matter the Home Office has demonstrated intolerance, ignorance, cowardice and an unwillingness to investigate complaints properly," he said.[21]

In the run-up to the 2010 election, the Scottish Conservative candidate, Philip Lardner, was deselected for expressing the view on his website that homosexuality was not "normal". This prompts the question whether it is any more possible for traditional Christian views to be held by politicians? Furthermore, it is now difficult to imagine any member of a future government publicly holding such conservative views on sexual morality. They must recant or face political oblivion. Elsewhere, MP Chris Grayling supported the right of Christian bed and breakfast owners in Cornwall who had refused a double bed to a gay couple. This may well have cost him a cabinet post after the general election. He was certainly compelled by the party leadership to apologize abjectly. Theresa May, Home Secretary at the time of writing, publicly repented of her "homophobic" voting record using the BBC programme, *Question Time*,

21 http://www.cmfblog.org.uk/2011/02/07/in-sacking-dr-raabe-the-home-office-has-demonstrated-intolerance-cowardice-and-ignorance/

as a "confessional" after 75,000 people joined a Facebook group calling for her sacking.

RELIGIOUS DISQUALIFICATION

In 2005, in the debate on Lord Joffe's euphemistically labelled bill on "assisted dying", secularist ire was levelled against the Church's opposition. In the House of Lords debate recorded in Hansard a number of speakers demonstrated a surprisingly hostile attitude towards the intervention by bishops and leaders of other faiths. There were even attempts to contrast the bigotry and zealotry of religious people with the superior compassion of the humanistic mindset. An exasperated bishop of Winchester intervened during Baroness Tonge's speech: "Is it her view – as it appears to be the view of others – that those who speak on these issues in the public domain from a position of religious faith are uniquely disqualified from doing so because that is among the positions from which they speak?" She disavowed that intention, but argued that "one cannot legislate for other people from a religious point of view".[22]

What an extraordinary argument! Simply because a proposal has a religious source it cannot be argued for in the public sphere. In fact, the religious arguments over assisted

---

22 http://www.publications.parliament.uk/pa/ld200506/ldhansrd/vo051010/text/51010-23.htm

dying and euthanasia rarely appeal solely to the Bible or any other sacred texts. Rather they hinge on a philosophical opposition to an absolute view of human autonomy. Although religious arguments are grounded in the absolute religious prohibition against killing, they appeal by way of evidence to the consequences of utilitarianism for society as a whole.

These examples make it absolutely clear that many secularists seek to deprive Christian believers of any sort of voice or role in public life.

FAITH AND WHOLENESS

When my predecessor, Archbishop Robert Runcie, and I ventured forth to defend the poor and powerless against unforeseen effects of government policy, we were often told to stop interfering with politics and stick to moralizing. Nowadays Church leaders are told to desist from both politicking and moralizing altogether. In 2011 when the Archbishop of Canterbury, Rowan Williams, expressed himself trenchantly in a guest editorial in the *New Statesman*, appearing to criticize aspects of the coalition policy in the areas of health, education, and welfare, he was told to stick to theology. Many commentators believe that he had no role in public life and should only address Christians with purely narrow doctrinal concerns. Of course, the irony was that only a month earlier he had conducted a Royal Wedding seen by billions around the globe which was in itself a highly "visible' and "political" act.

For Christians the whole of life is indivisible. We cannot retreat to a privatized ghetto because the gospel concerns the whole of life. There is no "privatized" morality because the whole of life is based on morality. Faith is necessarily public. The concerns of the Bible and theology throughout the ages have always been public and political. Our faith is intimately concerned not just with prohibitions surrounding sex, but with relationships, human wholeness, and well-being. The Bible addresses money, wealth, power, justice, environmental concerns, and many other aspects of modern life.

Believers cannot simply divest themselves of their faith when they enter politics or engage in public debate. The option outlined by Alastair Campbell, "We don't do God", is the stuff of censorship; it is not reflective of freedom of speech. Of course, a straightforward appeal to the Bible cannot convince those who do not believe. Yet religious adherents are entirely capable of constructing an argument based on rationality. Furthermore they have often earned the right to speak through experience and expertise. For example, in opposing euthanasia the Christian can point to palliative care and the hospice movement as a better way of dealing with pain and terminal illness at the end of life. The Christian involvement in hospices and the contribution of Christian medical professionals to palliative care is truly second-to-none. This is one very visible way in which the contribution of the Church to public debate through both its experience and teaching is profound and necessary.

CHAPTER SIX

CLASHING WITH THE LAW

This chapter highlights the clash between Christianity, the authorities, and the courts. It refers to a by no means exhaustive number of cases in which Christians have found themselves in conflict with those in authority above them. These authorities include local government, police, employers, and universities. Some of these cases involve fundamental issues of liberty and agency. Others concern allegations of homophobia. In some cases heavy-handed action by the authorities is averted when the issues are highlighted; in other cases they are resolved, often unhappily in the courts. The cases I mention are mostly the best-known cases, but there are many more in which issues of confidentiality apply.

Behind these stories lie a huge amount of anxiety and confusion among many Christians. Groups like Christian Concern and the Christian Institute receive many enquiries from churches and individuals seeking advice and guidance on negotiating a veritable minefield. The question of how to be a faithful disciple of Christ in often hostile environments challenges many ordinary Christians on a daily basis. Many resort to self-censorship for fear their views will be unpopular, controversial, or could lead to disciplinary action by employers. Others find themselves on the wrong side of authority and have to decide whether to take a stand or to back down quietly.

MARRIAGE AND FAMILY

Over recent years Christians with traditional views on homosexuality have sometimes found it difficult to complete fostering and adoption processes and have even had children taken away from them because of those views. The equality and diversity policies of local authorities state that the sexuality of children in care should be respected and this has often been interpreted to mean that potential foster-carers and adopters must agree that homosexual behaviour is acceptable and wholly support a child's choices to embrace such a lifestyle.

In a 2007 case, Vince and Pauline Matherick, who were long-time foster carers, found themselves in a dispute with

Somerset Social Services when they were asked to sign an equality policy.[23] After the case gained national press attention they received reassurances that signing the policy would not require them to act in any way that would compromise their consciences. Unfortunately in 2011 a court which was asked to adjudicate by Eunice and Owen Johns and Derby City Council on how to establish a balance between traditional Christian views and the council's diversity policies, appeared to establish the priority of equality over Christian conscience. Eunice and Owen Johns had previously fostered fifteen children for the council but found themselves investigated because of their Christian beliefs towards homosexuality. While they may still apply to the council to foster it looks extremely unlikely that the council will accept them in the light of the legal ruling. The couple said: "All we were not willing to do was to tell a small child that the practice of homosexuality was a good thing."[24]

Bill Beales, a highly respected comprehensive school head teacher, faced calls for his suspension after he told pupils in an assembly that Christians were being "placed on trial" for defending their beliefs on marriage.[25] The leader of the local council called for Beales' suspension despite the fact that his record as head teacher had led to dramatic improvements in the performance of the school.

23 "Victory for couple whose foster boy was taken away after they refused to promote gay relationships", *Daily Mail*, 2 November 2007.
24 "Foster parent ban: 'extreme distress' of 'anti-gay' Christians' over ruling", *Daily Telegraph*, 1 March 2011.
25 "Head defends evangelist speech", *BBC News*, 5 June 2002.

In 2007 Andrew McClintock lost his bid to have his freedom of conscience recognized when practising as a Justice of the Peace by an appeal court. In his role as a magistrate Mr McClintock felt that when the Civil Partnership Act was introduced in 2004 he would not be able to act in the best interests of a child by allowing them to be adopted by same sex couples. He asked to be "screened" from cases that might require him to act against his conscience.[26]

Christian registrars have also found themselves on the wrong side of the law when civil partnerships came into being. Lillian Ladele, an Islington registrar, sought permission from her employer to be excused from presiding over civil partnerships on the basis of Christian conscience. In December 2009 in a groundbreaking judgment, Ladele was refused permission to take her case to the Supreme Court (this case is explored further in Chapter Six).[27]

As mentioned in Chapter One, another famous appeal judgment that was rejected was the case of Gary McFarlane, a relationship counsellor from Bristol who was sacked by Relate after he refused to confirm that he would provide sex therapy to same sex couples.[28]

Dr Sheila Matthews was removed from the position of

---

26 "Christian magistrate in gay adoption row appeals against ruling", *Sunday Times*, 22 October 2007.
27 "Christian registrar denied leave to appeal gay wedding refusal", *Daily Telegraph*, 9 March 2010.
28 "Christian sex therapist Gary McFarlane loses appeal bid", *BBC News*, 29 April 2010.

medical advisor to Northamptonshire County Council's adoption panel after asking to abstain from voting on the "rare" occasion when same-sex couples wanted to adopt children.[29]

Even talking to colleagues about faith and sexual ethics could lead to disciplinary action, as charity worker, David Booker, found out. He was suspended under the "diversity rules" of the hostel in which he worked after answering a colleague's questions about his beliefs on sexual ethics. He was told that in expressing his views he broke the charity's "Culture and Diversity Code of Conduct".[30]

These cases demonstrate the inflexibility of equality and diversity guidelines when addressing issues of Christian conscience. It seems that negotiation and compromise can have no place in some workplaces where to even talk about one's views on morality can lead to discipline. Is this really the Orwellian world which supporters of such equality and diversity policies want to inhabit?

BANISHING FAITH

Although the European Convention on Human Rights protects the right of an individual to hold and manifest religious belief, there are an increasing number of cases in which Christians are being barred from talking about their faith or

29 "Christian advisor loses gay adoption care tribunal", *BBC News*, 16 November 2010.
30 "Charity worker suspended over 'religious debate' with work colleague", *Daily Telegraph*, 11 April 2009.

even from wearing religious symbols. In April 2008, figures for the previous twelve months showed 600 employees taking companies to a tribunal over religious discrimination – a significant increase from 486 cases two years earlier.[31]

In one of the most well-known cases, Nadia Eweida, a British Airways worker, was sent home when she refused to conceal a cross she was wearing. Her case gathered considerable support and under pressure BA eventually amended their uniform policy allowing employees to wear charitable or religious symbols. In 2010 she lost a claim for financial compensation for lost wages when a court ruled that BA were not guilty of religious discrimination. Also in 2010, Shirley Chaplin was faced with disciplinary action by her Devon NHS Trust for wearing a cross while at work as a nurse, despite having worn it to work for many years.[32]

Other cases involve employees who have been challenged for even talking about God in the workplace. In November 2009, Olive Jones was dismissed on the spot from her role as a supply teacher for offering to pray for a child and her family.[33]

Duke Amachree, a homelessness prevention officer for Wandsworth Council was dismissed for gross misconduct after suggesting to a client in poor health that she should

31 "Companies told to review rules to avoid 'indirect' religious discrimination", *Daily Telegraph*, 16 February 2009.
32 "Christian nurse loses battle to wear crucifix at work", *Guardian*, 6 April 2010.
33 "My ordeal, by Christian teacher fired for offering to pray for sick pupil", *Mail on Sunday*, 21 December 2008.

consider putting her faith in God.[34]

Caroline Petrie, a nurse from Weston-super-Mare was suspended without pay for simply asking a patient whether she would like to be prayed for.[35] She was suspended even though the patient in question did not report that she had taken offence. Petrie was told that she could face disciplinary action for a potential breach of the code of conduct on equality and diversity. Following representations and widespread media coverage she was eventually reinstated.

In 2011, at the time of writing this book, another member of the medical profession is seeking to clear his name after facing censure by the General Medical Council. Dr Richard Scott, one of six partners at a Kent medical centre that advertises itself as a Christian practice, was reported to the GMC for sharing his faith with a patient.

These cases reflect a society that is ill at ease with public expressions of faith. There is widespread ignorance about the nature of faith, a misconception that it can be consigned to a purely private place only to be brought out at Sunday worship – preferably behind the closed doors of a church. The Archbishop of York, John Sentamu, said in an interview in the *Daily Mail* in February 2009: "Asking someone to leave their belief in God at the door of their workplace is akin to asking them to remove their skin colour before

---

34 "Christian Wandsworth Council worker loses sacking claim", *BBC News*, 11 August 2010.
35 "Prayer nurse Caroline Petrie returns to work", *Daily Telegraph*, 23 February 2009.

coming into the office."[36]

In contrast the Liberal Democrat MP Lynne Featherstone suggested during the course of the passage of the Equality Act in 2010 that public sector workers with faith convictions should simply "make different choices about their careers".[37]

FREEDOM TO ASSOCIATE

There are signs that even the freedom to associate in worship can be challenged. In October 2009 a Kennington church was served a "noise abatement notice" banning the church from amplifying their music or sermons on threat of prosecution.[38] The All Nations Centre has been in its current location for over forty-five years but a small number of residents are reported to have begun complaining to the council about noise levels after the church conducted a leaflet drop in the local community.

Another church that was served with a noise abatement order by the local council was eventually able to come to an agreement with the council on volume limits.[39] The complaint was made by a Muslim neighbour who claimed

---

36 "The Intolerance towards Christians in the public sector is an affront", *Daily Mail*, 13 February 2009.
37 "Marginalising Christians, Instances of Christians being sidelined in Modern Britain", Christian Institute 2009.
38 "Churches ordered to 'sing softly'", *BBC News*, 20 October 2009.
39 "Church congregation dwindles after Muslim complaints", *Daily Telegraph*, 9 October 2009.

that the "noise" from the church prevented him using his garden at weekends.

In 2006 Exeter University Christian Union was suspended from the Guild of the Student Union because it required its members to sign a statement of faith.[40] The Student Union argued that the membership requirement discriminated against those who wanted to join the CU but could not sign the statement. I am aware of many other Christian Unions over the years that have faced similar difficulties.

POLICE AND PUBLIC ORDER

In a worrying number of cases police have taken action against street preachers. In August 2009 BBC Radio 4 highlighted the problems of police interference with the "long and honourable" tradition of street preaching and asked if street preachers were victims of "intolerance". The report included a recording of an incident where the Open-Air Mission evangelist Andy Robertson was told by police officers that it is a criminal offence to identify homosexuality as a sin. Mr Robertson had made no mention of homosexuality in his preaching.

Julian Hurst was handing out leaflets to the public in Manchester, inviting people to Easter services when a man complained to police that he was offended on grounds of

---

40 "Exeter CU threaten legal action over 'ban'", *Guardian*, 17 November 2006.

his sexual orientation. The inoffensive leaflet was entitled "New Life, Fresh Hope". Mr Hurst was visited in his home by a PC from the Race and Hate Crime unit who confirmed that Mr Hurst was within his rights to distribute the leaflet on public streets. The very fact that the police were forced to take this time-wasting complaint seriously is surely a cause for concern?

In February 2008, a police community support officer told two church workers in Birmingham that they could not preach because they were in a Muslim area.[41] They were told that they were committing a hate crime. One of the officers said, "You have been warned. If you come back here and get beat up, well you have been warned."

In 2008 Tony Rollins was arrested after preaching in Birmingham on same-sex relationships. He was arrested under Section 5 of the Public Order Act, handcuffed, and kept in a police cell for four hours. Mr Rollins suffers from Asperger's syndrome. After representations the Crown Prosecution Service decided the case was not in the public interest.[42]

Street preaching has also come under interference from various councils in recent years. An official from Carlisle Council told Keith Bullock, a Christian evangelist with Open-Air Mission that he could not hand out Christian literature in the city centre without the Council's permission. The Council was acting under a misunderstanding of the laws

41 "You can't preach the Bible here, this is a Muslim area", *Daily Mail*, 2 June 2008.
42 "Case dropped against 'anti-gay' preacher Tony Rollins", *Birmingham Mail*, 12 September 2008.

which prevent littering, but which do not apply to political or religious literature. The council later apologized.[43]

ESTABLISHING THE CASE

It is probably a forlorn hope that common sense would simply reassert itself in the light of these often grievous examples of discrimination outlined above. What we should not fail to note is the speed in which there has been a seismic shift in the way Christian behaviour is now seen and interpreted. We live in a civilization which, in no small way, has been marked and shaped by Christianity and Christian ethics. We have a monarch who is Supreme Governor of the Church of England and we have a Parliament that begins its sessions with prayer in both Houses. Yet, here we are today where to be a public Christian may entail loss of work and even jail if you are faithful to your convictions.

I fear however that we will see many more cases of this kind in the years ahead. The danger is that the public will become so desensitized to the continual reporting of these stories that they will no longer shock. Often media coverage is one way of ensuring that these incidents reach a satisfactory conclusion.

There is, however, a worrying trajectory in many of these cases, that when they reach the courts Christians cannot

43 "Carlisle Council apologises", *Evangelical Times*, April 2007.

possibly win. We must now address the weighty issues raised when some of these cases have been in the hands of lawyers and judges.

CHRISTIAN FREEDOM AND THE LAW

Christians have lost their livelihoods, have been investigated by police, and have encountered environments in which they are unable to wear a cross or even talk about their faith. Many of these cases involved competing rights and have invited the courts to adjudicate too often with disastrous consequences for believers.

It must not be forgotten that it is in little more than a decade of successive developments in law, and especially the extension of equality laws, that Britain has become a much colder place for religious conscience. In some senses the incorporation of the Human Rights Act in 1998 can be said to have been the starting point. This was followed by waves of equality regulations, including the notorious Sexual Orientation Regulations (SORS). The advent of the Civil Partnerships Act in 2004 posed particular problems for many Christians. And lastly the Equality Act 2010 became the one-stop shop for all previous legislation, setting out to be a tidying-up exercise, but actually widening the scope of equality legislation and progressively narrowing religious exemptions.

This alarming amount of legislation in a very short space of time has resulted in the creation of a hierarchy of rights. For Christians, the most obvious effect has been in the competition between their rights and those of sexual minorities.

RELIGIOUS FREEDOM

Rights to freedom of religious conscience have been hard fought for throughout Europe, let alone in Britain. A tragic aspect of the history of the Church of England has been the uniformity imposed in previous centuries, and the persecution that ensued. Catholicism, Puritanism, and Nonconformism have been variously suppressed and persecuted. Yet as a result of this history the framers of the European Convention on Human Rights gave a high priority to religious freedom in Article 9. This emerged as the right to freedom of thought, conscience, and religion most importantly granting the believer the right to manifest "his religion or belief in worship, teaching, practice and observance".

All rights are of course qualified when they brush up against those of others, but the limitations in Article 9 are narrow. Commentators have pointed out that freedom of religion is one of the least qualified rights in the Convention.

However, as it has turned out in the course of parliamentary debates on equality and diversity, many lawmakers seem keen to confine freedom of believers to manifesting their faith to the private sphere alone. Equality legislation was deemed to pass the religious freedom test solely on the grounds that it did not constrain believers in holding their opinions personally or from worshipping freely. As we have seen, though, the moment when religious views are uttered out loud, or Christians seek wriggle room in their employment conditions for freedom of conscience, that "manifestation of belief" is severely circumscribed.

RELIGIOUS ILLITERACY

This demonstrates an illiteracy regarding religious faith that is all too prevalent. To restrict religious manifestation to the private sphere or to apply it purely to worship in church buildings, is no kind of religious liberty at all. Christians cannot hang up their faith as they enter the workplace. Thus a culture war has arisen out of primary legislation, which has been left to the courts to settle. And indeed the courts have gone about their business on an unfortunate trajectory that appears on the face of it to have left religious believers at the bottom of the heap.

A fundamental confusion for both the courts and the lawmakers is a misunderstanding of traditional Christian expressions of morality. Christians, like everybody else, believe that sexual minorities are equal but they do not believe that all expressions of sexuality are equally acceptable. This, of course, is a distinction which homosexuals, in particular, cannot accept. There is no possible way of squaring this circle. Just as Christians believe that the whole of life is indivisible and that their faith cannot be pushed into a purely private space, so many homosexuals cannot live with a distinction which separates orientation and behaviour. This inevitable clash of world views would in previous times have been picked up in the legislative process rather than being left to an adversarial court system.

In the 1967 Abortion Act considerable thought was given to the protection of the rights and consciences of Christian medical care workers. Similarly under the Sunday Trading laws legislation could not have proceeded without a guarantee for Christians to be able to attend their places of worship. There was no such preparatory work when Civil Partnerships came into being in 2004. It was completely obvious that a small number of Christian registrars and others, who had performed their work well in the past, would now be faced with a crisis of conscience. Yet the time for exemptions, negotiation, and compromise had come to an end and it was now left to the courts to settle such conflicts. It must be argued that the primary responsibility for these increasingly ill-tempered clashes between competing sets of rights should be fairly laid at the door of Parliament, which has rushed legislation to the statute book with little thought for unintended consequences. Many politicians and commentators now believe that the courts have become an over-mighty rival to parliamentary power. If this is the case, then the lawmakers have only themselves to blame.

LEGAL DECISIONS

We must turn now to the most troubling aspects of some of these legal judgments. The case of Lillian Ladele versus the London Borough of Islington is a highly publicized case that appears to have established important precedents in the legal system. Ladele was a Christian registrar who asked her employers to excuse her from conducting civil partnership ceremonies. After a refusal of this request and disciplinary action by Islington against her, she brought a case for religious discrimination. In this case it was quite clear that Ladele was not seeking to undermine Islington's policies but merely seeking to put some of her new duties in the hands of other registrars who had no such crisis of conscience. This could so easily have been resolved by negotiation but instead the council resorted to disciplinary action claiming that to make an exception for Ladele was to undermine their public duties on equality. In her witness statement she said,

"Regardless of my feelings for the participants (and as a Christian this should only be love), I feel unable to directly facilitate the formation of a union that I sincerely believe is contrary to God's law."[44]

Ladele initially won her case in a tribunal with the key finding being that Ladele's beliefs were put at a disadvantage. Furthermore, the tribunal stated that Islington Council had not shown that the disciplinary proceedings against Ladele were a "proportionate means of achieving the legitimate aim of promoting the rights" of homosexuals.

On appeal, the claims of discrimination were overturned when the Employment Appeal Tribunal ruled that the council had not acted against Ladele on the grounds of her religious belief, but because of her conduct. They held that since she was not being treated differently from other employees, the council could not be held to be guilty of direct discrimination. Later Appeal Court judgments reinforced this position, but also emphasized the limitations on religious freedom provided by equality law and the passing of Sexual Orientation Regulations in 2007.

This curious line of reasoning began to permeate other judgments. A telling statement from the Court of Appeal in the appeal tribunal judgment of Ladelle outlined the argument: "If I burn down my employer's factory because of my philosophical anarchist beliefs, an employer who

---

44 "Christian registrar 'threatened with sack' after refusing to conduct gay marriage", *Evening Standard*, 21 May 2008.

dismisses me thereafter for burning down the factory is not doing so because of my philosophical beliefs. Those beliefs may be the reason for my action, but they are not the reason for the employers' response."[45]

From one point of view this argument appears to be entirely valid: it is action that determines the sentence. Belief led to unacceptable behaviour. But in the case of both Eweida and Ladele, it was the action of their employer that determined the sentence. What was once acceptable practice in the UK for hundreds of years – the right to wear a cross at work and to express one's disapproval of homosexual practice – was now denied them. Both Eweida and Ladele were simply following their practice as they had always done. Neither wished to become a "cause célèbre" but their conscience dictated that they must follow through what they regarded as morally right. In the case of Ladele, the Court of Appeal stated that marriage was not a core value of Christianity and therefore Ladele was being unreasonable. What right has a secular court to determine centrality of practice to a faith? Marriage is as central to Ladele's faith as it is to mine, and to the majority of Christians. In the case of Eweida the court determined that she was not required to wear the cross because that is not mandatory in the Christian faith. While that is so, the importance of the cross is that it is so central that, while individuals are not compelled to wear it, to compel a Christian *not* to wear it (because someone else has

---

45 Elias J. in the EAT decision in Ladele, para 55.

concluded that it is not important) is to raise the stakes and force them to deny their faith. It is to challenge the human rights of another.

There is some imbalance in legal outcomes in this area as the law applies to other faiths. My attention, for example, has been drawn to the case of Watkins Singh where the High Court upheld the claimant's right to wear the Sidra Kara to school, even though she was not obliged by her religion to wear it.[46] Though Watkins Singh was decided under Race laws there is some similarity.

CAREY VS LAWS

It was clear that an impasse was being reached in a succession of court judgments in which freedom of religious conscience was held to be secondary to equality requirements resulting in severe hardship to individual Christians. I was asked to provide a supporting witness statement to Gary McFarlane, the Relate counsellor mentioned earlier, who was claiming that he was discriminated against by his employers, Relate by being refused to excuse himself from giving sexual counselling to homosexual couples. He was dismissed for gross misconduct. An employment tribunal ruled that while he had not been unfairly dismissed, he had indeed been

---

46 "'Proud to be Welsh and a Sikh' Schoolgirl wins Court battle to wear religious bangle", *Guardian*, 30 July 2008.

"wrongfully" dismissed. However in the Appeal courts, like Ladele, he fared badly.[47]

In my witness statement to the Court of Appeal presided over by Lord Justice Laws, I argued that past rulings against Christians had misunderstood religious objections and the basis upon which religious manifestation was formed. I therefore called for special training for the judges to guard against the religious illiteracy that the courts were displaying. It had become clear that while the courts pretended to be neutral on religious questions they had come close at times to trespassing on matters that belong to the realm of theology, especially in rulings which were held to decide on the importance for individual Christians of wearing a cross, or where specious reasoning had led them to declare that opinions on sexual ethics and marriage did not concern "core doctrines" of the Christian faith.

I urged the Appeal Court to create a small panel of judges who had training or understanding of religious faith, to rule in the Appeal Court on issues of religious freedom and liberty where they clashed with other rights.

Lord Justice Laws' response to my witness statement was withering and scornful. He acknowledged that laws in Britain have been influenced by the Christian faith, saying: "The Judeo-Christian tradition, stretching over many centuries, has no doubt exerted a profound influence upon the judgment

---

47 "Christian sex therapist Gary McFarlane loses appeal bid", *BBC News*, 29 April 2010.

of lawmakers as to the objective merits of this or that social policy." But then he issued a stinging attack on my argument stating that it would be "deeply unprincipled" to confer "any legal protection or preference upon a particular substantive moral position... however long its tradition". Lord Justice Laws went on to state – rather than argue – that "in the eye of everyone, save the believer, religious faith is necessarily subjective, being incommunicable by any kind of proof or evidence... it lies only in the heart of the believer, who alone is bound by it. No one else can be so bound, unless by his own free choice he accepts its claims. The promulgation of law for the protection of a position held purely on religious grounds cannot therefore be justified. It is irrational, as preferring the subjective over the objective. But it is also divisive, capricious and arbitrary."

Most problematic of all was his contention that any particular status for religion within the law led in the direction of "theocracy". This was, of course, to ignore the fact that religious identity is already a "protected characteristic" and that exemptions for religious believers have been granted on a whole range of matters. Furthermore, the establishment of the Church of England itself in Britain's constitution indicates that there can be a halfway house between a purely secular state and a theocracy. The Church of England is by law established and in some sense at least, this demonstrates that the law itself privileges and gives preference to a particular manifestation of faith.

His contention that "laws for the protection of a position held purely on religious grounds is irrational, divisive, capricious and arbitrary" is equally troubling. He seems to assume that religious conscience itself is purely personal and cannot be argued for on rational grounds in the public sphere. Furthermore, such religious arguments can contribute to both lawmaking and judicial interpretation. That which counts as "rational, and objective and conducive to the common good" does not come about by means of a secular version of the Ten Commandments handed out from on high, but through democratic negotiation, and dispute. As is most evident from my appeal to the Court on behalf of McFarlane, I was not arguing for special treatment for Christians, or seeking to establish a "theocratic" state. I was appealing for judges to have an understanding of religious issues because it has become palpably obvious that judges appear to be unaware of basic issues relating to the Christian faith.

The argument for a specialist bench of judges to hear a particular type of case is well known in law (there are administrative judges, commercial judges, family judges) and in the light of recent judgments it was a wholly sensible proposition.

It seems clear from Lord Justice Laws' judgment that he is unaware of his opinion that religious belief is purely "subjective", "incommunicable by any kind of proof or evidence", can equally be applied to any expression of opinion even his own.

In June 2011 the European Court of Human Rights began to take an interest in rulings by British courts on issues of religious rights.[48] A request from the Strasbourg courts called for a statement from the British government to clarify whether the rights of Christians have been infringed, after Nadia Eweida, Gary McFarlane, Shirley Chaplin and Lillian Ladele applied to the court for the review.

Such a statement from the government may have some effect in clearing up the confusion that has been created by both Parliament and the courts in recent times. Interestingly, the European Court has recently ruled rather more favourably than the British system on religious freedom, upholding for example Italy's right to display crucifixes in its classrooms.

It is therefore very clear that something is deeply wrong in some legal interpretation of laws referring to human rights. It is manifestly obvious that homosexual rights trump religious rights.

In short, the situation is now extremely serious. The result of the equalities legislation (regarding religion or belief and sexual orientation) which came into force from 2003 has actually led to discrimination against Christians, depriving them of equality under the law compared to others. The

48 "European court intervenes over rights of Christians", *Christianity Today*, 6 June 2011.

editorial of the *Daily Telegraph* of 19 January 2011 put it well: "The right to hold religious beliefs, and to act in keeping with one's faith, is being set against the right not to offend – and is losing. This is a dispiriting trend in a free society." Some balance is required which will reassure Christian believers, who are still in a majority in this country, that they have employment rights and that these rights are respected. If the courts are now unable to protect the now considerable numbers of people who have lost their right to practice their beliefs, then Parliament should do so.

CHAPTER 7

THE ROOTS OF CONFLICT

The Church is no longer the powerful and central body it was, but neither is it weak and helpless. True, institutional faith is shrinking and in some parts of the UK Islam has more practising adherents than Christianity. But there is a silent majority who respect the role of the Church and whose commitment to it is evident on public occasions. However, the story we have depicted so far in this book reveals that the Church is being sidelined, and some Christians brave enough to follow their convictions are suffering as a result. The question we must ask is: What difference is it making to Christians and if the results are negative, what can we do about it?

At the beginning of 2011 Prime Minister David Cameron told the nation of his desire to use the energies of community to create a "Big Society" which will deepen community and create a more caring nation. If David Cameron's vision of the Big Society is to produce any long-lasting effects on Britain, as he clearly hopes, it cannot ignore the enormous contribution brought to the table by churches and Christian charities. In reality, governments of all complexions have always acknowledged the role of faith groups in the provision of social services, even if they have sometimes undervalued this contribution.

In every neighbourhood in Britain the churches are playing some kind of role in building the common good. They maintain buildings that are used by the whole neighbourhood, run parents and toddlers groups, parenting courses, lunch clubs for the elderly, and social events to unite the community. There are many church community centres, youth clubs, advice centres, and credit unions. Congregations now undertake audits to see how they can best meet the needs of the area in which they are situated. They faithfully serve on soup runs, offer their facilities to the homeless, and provide hostels for the homeless. On top of all this activity, Christians also give their money, often generously, not just to maintain the fabric of their own buildings and pay the stipends of their ministers, but to overseas relief charities and many home-grown causes. They volunteer their time as school governors, in the Citizens Advice Bureau, and in many local charities. Church buildings now increasingly host post offices and shops for isolated communities. On an everyday basis, clergy and church workers visit the sick and disabled maintaining a link with those who could otherwise become isolated and lonely. This is a remarkable and often ignored story. As we have seen, it has not been ignored by Roy Hattersley, an atheist, who concluded after the flooding of New Orleans, where American churches responded to the plight of the poor with amazing generosity, that faith did indeed breed charity. "The correlation is so clear that it is impossible to doubt that faith and charity go hand in hand," he wrote. He bemoaned the fact that when disasters happened it wasn't groups of atheists who came to the rescue but Christians.[49]

Pity indeed the State that is prepared to squander such social capital. The opportunities for partnership with the Christian voluntary sector and the churches are enormous. Yet in such a cold climate for contribution of distinctively Christian bodies, the potential has arisen instead for mutual suspicion and antipathy.

I don't envisage for a moment the churches withdrawing from loving their neighbours, which after all is the commitment and obedience behind their efforts. Nevertheless, partnership could be soured and spoilt if the State continues to set bureaucratic obstacles and diversity criteria at too high a level. In a time of spending cuts when society needs these initiatives ever more, many charities are failing to gain necessary funding. The vast majority of Christian initiatives

---

49 "Faith does breed charity", *Guardian*, 12 September 2005.

do not require State funding, but those that do often have to downplay their Christian ethos. Christian nursing homes, for example, which are badly needed in an ageing society, have lost their funding. In one case, Pilgrim Homes a 200-year-old Christian charity (set up by William Wilberforce and others) received an annual grant from Brighton Council for its elderly care home in the city. In 2007 the council pulled the grant and accused the home of "homophobia" after the charity refused to comply with demands that it should regularly question residents about their sexuality, publicize LGBT events, force staff to attend a presentation by the homosexual advocacy organization Stonewall, and use images of homosexual couples in its promotional literature. Under the threat of legal action the council restored the funding.

The very fact that a number of former Roman Catholic adoption agencies have been forced to break links with the church in order to continue in their role is a cause for considerable concern. The weakening of their ethos may be far more threatening to their long-term future than the funding issues. The very success of church schools is an indicator that being rooted in a Christian community is a key indicator of good results.

SOCIAL PARIAHS

We are also in danger of reaching a point at which people who would previously have been considered pillars of the community have now reached the status of social pariahs. The very fact that some Christians may find it hard to make a contribution to fostering children in the light of legal judgments is a massive waste. The choice now facing many is to be silent about their beliefs in order to continue working in the public sector, or simply to find jobs elsewhere.

The cases I have highlighted in previous chapters often tell a story of people happily going about their daily lives, wearing their faith openly and comfortably, and who used to confidently play a full part in society. In the course of one conversation, or one event, or because of one single complaint, their lives are then changed. Some of them have lost their livelihoods, others have been distressed by unexpected interventions by heavy-handed employers or authorities. Increasing numbers of Christians feel anxious, uncomfortable, and frightened of participating fully in public life as a result of these stories. We are in danger of alienating and excluding them through a combination of well-meaning political correctness, ignorance, and sometimes even an outright hostility to the expression of religious belief.

The effect of a combination of new legislation and judicial activism has been to hurt individual believers, diminish the status of the Church and alter the relationship of many Christians to the State.

TOLERANCE – A FORGOTTEN VIRTUE?

Behind this confused state of affairs there rests confusion about the place of tolerance in modern Britain. Is there any room for principled dissent in our "liberal democracy"? In allowing different opinions to exist side by side, have we unknowingly moved from acceptance of certain practices to that of insisting that formerly held minority opinions are now the only ones that are allowed to exist? As Professor Brenda Almond of the University of Hull put it: "The transition from the pre-Wolfenden position when society punished as a crime private conduct of which it disapproved, has progressed to a point where disapproval of it has become a modern heresy. Tolerance, it seems, has been turned on its head. Such changes have resulted in Christians being forced to make a choice between their professions and their conscience."[50]

However, sometimes the endeavour to be seen to be as tolerant as possible has serious unintended consequences. In 2009 parents of a school in Waltham Forest found themselves in a bizarre situation when they withdrew their children from school to keep them from attending a compulsory week of

50 *Journal of Moral Education*, Vol. 39, No. 2, June 2010, p. 139.

special lessons to highlight lesbian, gay, and transgender partnerships. The aim was to promote tolerance in their schools and to teach that all people are of equal value. The protesting parents, who included Christians and Muslims, were warned that their action could contravene the law and merit prosecution. Tolerance, it seems, is a one-way street. However, true tolerance in a nation must give space for different expressions of belief as well as behaviour. Currently, lawmakers and judges are creating an inevitable conflict for religious believers who are being forced to choose between compliance and conscience. By insisting on compliance on matters that are morally questionable in the eyes of some citizens, the State is moving beyond democracy to authoritarianism and thus creating an unhealthy culture.

OLD-TIME RELIGION

The intervention of the Equality and Human Rights Commission with a landmark report on religious discrimination, seemed to confirm these fears of a one-way street in matters to do with tolerance. In an interview with the *Sunday Telegraph* newspaper, Trevor Phillips, Chairman of the Commission, criticized Christian fundamentalism and "old-time" religion on the part of the Afro-Caribbean community for not integrating into the mainstream.[51]

51 Article published 18 June 2011.

The problem he suggested arose from those of his own background, "We like our faith strong and pretty undiluted. If you come from an Afro-Caribbean Christian background the attitudes to homosexuality are unambiguous, they are undiluted, they are nasty and in some cases homicidal."

The noise, he suggested, about "persecution" arose from those who believe in an "old-time" religion which "in my view is incompatible with a modern, multi-ethnic, multicultural society". In contrast he suggested, the Muslim community is doing their best to integrate. The most likely victim of actual religious discrimination was a Muslim, but the person most likely to feel slighted was an evangelical Christian, he argued.

And the reason that Christians feel slighted? It's simple, he explained, "It's about politics. It's about a group of people who really want to have weight and influence and they've chosen that particular ground."

While Phillips pledged to preserve religious liberty, and defended faith from the over-the-top atheistic attacks which have become commonplace, his statements reveal a considerable misunderstanding. I know from my experience of being in contact with a number of people who have found themselves on the wrong side of the law on these matters, that they are not seeking political power, nor a Christian theocracy, nor any disadvantage to any other community. They are asking for a level playing field. The suggestion is that their rights should not be superior to anyone else's but essentially the same. In fact, in a period of turbulent change where the equality laws have changed dramatically in a very short space of time, they are simply asking for the rights they had previously taken for granted in the past five or ten years to continue to be protected.

Phillips is also ignoring, like so many others, the essentially Christian nature of this country, with its lingering traces of a uniquely Christian constitution. The very idea, that Christians of an Afro-Caribbean background with a principled theological opposition to homosexual practice, are somehow guilty of "extremism" or the practice of "power politics" is both deeply insulting and utterly untrue, as I know from personal experience. The worst that can be said, is that like many other Christians they are bewildered by the sheer rate of change. Those who have a first or perhaps even second generation experience of British life seem more acutely aware than many others, how hostile the climate for Christianity has actually become. The reaction of such Christians is far from a power-grab, it is rather one of despair.

IS THIS PERSECUTION?

I am well aware from my mail bag that many Christians are asking whether they any longer have a place in modern society? Are they debarred from certain professions? Will

Christianity be increasingly frozen out of the public sphere by draconian overreaction?

These are important questions. From what I have described we have every reason to be concerned, but we have to remind ourselves that the plight of Christians in the West does not even remotely compare to places of the world where Christians face persecution. To their situation we must now turn.

In 1995, on my way to Sudan, I spent a few hours in a country where to all intents and purposes, Christianity is banned. I regarded my pastoral visit to the suffering Sudanese Church as absolutely vital, so against my better judgment, I allowed myself to be persuaded to enter Saudi Arabia without collar or cross. I was told I risked not being able to continue to Sudan if I did not conform to the oppressive Saudi laws.

At the British compound, I had agreed to take a service for Christians of all denominations from the various embassies in the vicinity, but I had no idea of the problems this had caused. Christian worship was forbidden and the service was advertised as a meeting of the "Welfare Committee (P&C)" – with the initials standing for Protestants and Catholics. The hall was packed with all denominations. As I led Evening Prayer and preached, I was moved by the feeling that this act of worship had many parallels with the earliest days of the persecuted New Testament Church. Immediately after the service, the convenor of the "Welfare Committee" urged everyone to go straight to their cars, so as not to raise suspicions. Yet I was told that in spite of these restrictions and the penalties imposed by the authorities, Christianity was flourishing in the kingdom.

I have visited many other countries where the practice of Christian worship is either circumscribed by law, or by the antipathy and hostility of communities. In Nigeria, the adoption of sharia law in some northern states has harmed the Christian community leading to what is often described in the media as "inter-communal violence". In reality that is usually a euphemism for fanatical and savage Islamist attacks on Christians and the burning of church buildings.

In Pakistan, the operation of that country's blasphemy laws has led to many deaths in the Christian community. Those who are usually falsely accused of insulting the prophet or defacing the Qu'ran are often the victims of unscrupulous people who are using the law to settle personal disputes. I made many visits to Sudan; in the south (as of July 2011, officially a separate country), I visited Christian communities upon which war had been waged for decades; in the north, the Anglican cathedral in Khartoum was confiscated by the government.

In India, who can forget the Australian missionary, Graham Staines, who was burnt to death by Hindu extremists in his station wagon together with his two sons Philip (aged ten) and Timothy (aged six) while they were sleeping in his vehicle?

He is not the only Christian martyr of the modern age. In 1998 a frieze marking twentieth-century martyrs, which I dedicated, was unveiled before the Queen at Westminster Abbey. Carefully selected to represent a wide range of international figures, they included the famous and celebrated such as Martin Luther King, Saint Elizabeth of Russia, Archbishop Oscar Romero, Archbishop Janani Luwum and Dietrich Bonhoeffer. Manche Masemola, an Anglican catechumen from South Africa who was killed in 1928 by her parents at the age of sixteen is also remembered at Westminster Abbey, as is Esther John, a Presbyterian evangelist from Pakistan.

At the service commemorating these figures, Anthony Harvey, the sub-dean of Westminster Abbey, pointed to the twentieth century as the most violent in recorded history, creating a roll of Christian martyrs far exceeding that of any previous period. "There has never been a time in Christian history when someone, somewhere, has not died rather than compromise with the powers of oppression, tyranny and unbelief," he said.

The twenty-first century could well be even bloodier than its predecessor if the genocide in Darfur, and violence against Christians in many other countries is anything to go by. Christians in Britain should therefore never cease to remember the martyrs of the past, and support their brothers and sisters elsewhere in the world who are suffering much more severe forms of oppression and persecution than we are ever likely to experience.

This is why I have never used the word "persecution" to refer to the plight of Christians experiencing difficulties in Britain, and western Europe. While I have detailed in the previous chapters a catalogue of injustices experienced by individual Christians, even to the point of losing their livelihoods and jobs, and while we have observed an encroaching of the State on the governance of churches and religious bodies, together with a judicial activism which has subordinated the rights of believers to that of other minorities, nevertheless we continue to enjoy great freedom. Church building is allowed unhampered by anything but the usual planning and construction laws. Church schools are among the most successful and widespread in our state education system. The Church of England is established and bishops still sit in the House of Lords. On a local level, the churches have significant roles in Remembrance Sunday, in civic ceremonies, and in the lives of communities throughout the land. Christians continue to serve the nation, run charities, contribute responsibly to society in a huge variety of roles. There are no constraints on our worship, on our basic freedoms. Most of us will never encounter a prejudice more severe than the occasional sneer.

In his 2010 Easter letter, the current Archbishop of Canterbury, Rowan Williams, made a similar observation that in a wide variety of places worldwide, actual persecution, attacks, and communal violence against Christians are taking place. He wrote: "When St John tells us that the disciples met behind locked doors on the first Easter Day (John 20:19), he reminds us that being associated with Jesus Christ has never been easy or safe."

We need to keep our own fears in perspective, he said. In his 2010 Easter sermon he went on to criticize "overheated language" used to describe Christian suffering in Britain, arguing that "wooden-headed bureaucratic silliness" combined with a "well-meaning and completely misplaced anxiety about giving offence to non-Christians should not be mistaken for persecution".[52]

It seems likely that these overblown claims of "Christian persecution" in Britain may be behind the squeamishness of Steve Clifford, the general director of the Evangelical Alliance, towards the Gary McFarlane appeal. He wrote that when Christians paint a portrait of persecution we diminish the very real suffering that our fellow believers across the world experience. However, Mr Clifford went further and argued that Christians themselves were forcing themselves to the margins. "If Christians are marginalized in the UK, then we have to take at least some of the blame," he wrote.[53]

---

52 "Rowan Williams condemns 'overheated language' used to describe Christian suffering", *Guardian*, 5 April 2010.
53 Comment, *Independent*, 20 April, 2010.

How seriously do we take his warning that some of our rhetoric is itself contributing to the situation of Christians in Britain today? Could it be that we are getting our just desserts after centuries of dominating British society and that our current problems are merely those of a society in transition towards a new way of negotiating between communities of Christians and the larger community of non-believers?

There may be some truth in these claims. Words like "persecution" and "oppression" are words to rally the troops rather than to constructively engage in society. The director of the Evangelical Alliance and the Archbishop of Canterbury are both right to warn against waging war with such words. There is a real risk that we will not be taken seriously, and that we will paint ourselves into a corner from which there is both no retreat and no way forward.

However, many church leaders have offered nothing but silence to the plight of Christians who are directly experiencing hardship, or to communities which seek to challenge deliberate bureaucratic attempts to sideline Christianity, or heavy-handed policing. They are right to call for a constructive engagement with the authorities, but what counsel do leaders offer to Christians who have lost their jobs for wearing a cross, or when they find that new policies conflict with their consciences? Should the Christian nurse instructed to take off her cross meekly comply with those demands? Should a Christian teacher suspended for offering a prayer to a pupil just simply walk away with this blot on his or her employment record?

It seems that too often the response is "tough luck". Church leaders have largely kept silent as tribunals and courts have ruled against the free exercise of Christian conscience in employment. I doubt that they are suggesting that Christians should never, under any circumstances, resort to the law in a clear case of injustice. I cannot believe that they are suggesting that for the sake of cohesion in society Christians should never stand up for their own rights. So what are Christian leaders saying? And why are they so unwilling to publicly give their backing to people caught up in very real crises of conscience and hardship like Lillian Ladelle or Gary McFarlane?

Mr Clifford laments the extent to which Christians find themselves in court these days. "Whether it is to keep our job, wear religious symbols or over freedom to preach and pray, the role of Christianity in public life is no longer straightforward, though I doubt it ever was."

He argues that the courts cannot enforce stability and tolerance. And in fact every court case creates a greater disconnect between the Church and society. "Christians do not need to pick a fight with the society they inhabit," he adds.

Sadly, Mr Clifford is not the only Church leader who has failed to grasp that in the vast majority of cases it is not

Christians who are picking a fight – they are on the receiving end. Should we relinquish the right to free speech? Should we abandon the right of churches to employ ministers who conform to deeply held convictions of faith? Should the Roman Catholic adoption agencies have closed down, or have gone independent from the Church without a word of dissent? Should we meekly bow down before the social pressures of conformity, take off our crosses, and keep our faith in a private box sealed off from our work colleagues with the status of an embarrassing secret?

No one enters into litigation willingly unless they happen to be a lawyer. But in the cases I have been supporting, hardworking and skilled people have sought to negotiate with their employers and have finally found that they have no choice. There are many more who go quietly, leave their employment, and seek other jobs. Others manage to come to some form of compromise with their employers, including one doctor who wanted to absent herself from adoption panels when same-sex couples were the adoptees. Her employer, a local authority, valued her expertise so highly that her terms were quietly accepted. Yet in other cases, the employers are so intractable and hostile to faith claims that their Christian employees have had to resort to law. It is a right that should be defended.

The Bible of course looks askance at litigation in some contexts. In fact to use the adversarial system of the courts in disputes over employment and other matters is always a second best to negotiation and mediation. In 1 Corinthians 6:1–8 Paul famously tells the Corinthians not to go to court against each other. The Gospel of Matthew seems to indicate that the early church quickly developed a pattern for dealing with disputes: "If your brother sins against you, go and show him his fault, just between the two of you. If he listens to you, you have won your brother over. But if he will not listen then take one or two others along, so that 'every matter may be established by the testimony of two or three witnesses.' If he refuses to listen to them, tell it to the church; and if he refuses to listen even to the church, treat him as you would a pagan or a tax collector" (Matthew 18:15–17).

The passing reference to pagans and tax collectors does not give us carte blanche to resort to litigation in civil matters either. The pattern of seeking a resolution outside the adversarial court system is a matter of being the best witness to Jesus Christ, and a display of the fruits of the Spirit, which include qualities such as long-suffering and love. Nevertheless, St Paul does seem to indicate that settling matters in courts is an option for things which don't concern church life. When Paul is arrested and wrongfully accused of a crime (Acts 21–22) the Roman commander orders a whipping with lashes to make him confess his crime. Paul questions the officer on whether it is legal to whip a Roman citizen who hasn't been tried. It is clear that on a matter of human rights the courts are there to protect us from injustice.

Nevertheless, while I have been critical of church leaders for their failure to grasp the seriousness of the situation, nevertheless I believe we should tone down the rhetoric and, like Steve Clifford, plead for every other avenue to be explored first before the courts. The role of the Church and the individual Christian in society after all is to be a witness to the love of Christ, not an advocate for a shrill and selfish culture of victimhood.

It is important for Christians to downplay the language of spiritual warfare. As they do so, they will find that they are not alone, and that many non-churchgoers are equally incensed by the downplaying of Christmas, Easter, nativity plays and so on, the marginalization of the Christian faith, and individual incidents of injustice. After all, encroachments from the State on churches also affect other organizations. Britons are used to thinking of themselves as free, fair, and decent. A fundamentalist secularism, or a doctrinaire political-correctness offends British sensibilities far more than a courageous and courteous statement of Christian values.

We are not at war with society; our problems are with a few employers, a Human Rights Act which seems to downgrade the rights of Christians, and the tendency of governments to emphasize the virtues of an over-mighty State. And in fact while the rhetoric of persecution and warfare in the short term will rally the faithful, in the long term it will tend to lead to retreat and disengagement.

The nature of our dialogue is not to withdraw in a fit of pique but to engage in a positive manner with all criticism. We cannot and must not engage with people as enemies, but as friends whom we seek to persuade by the quality of our arguments and our general witness of love. In the debate on assisted suicide the bishops were roundly criticized for foisting a Christian morality on the rest of the population. Nevertheless they continued to politely and intelligently mount a case against assisted suicide based not on texts from the Bible, but through a serious engagement with their opponents, addressing the limits to human autonomy and the effects that changes to the law could have on families and the doctor–patient relationship. They won the argument by refusing to be driven out of the public square and continuing to engage on the same terms with those who refused to hear them.

The churches have a valuable history of constructive engagement in Britain from the founding of our education system, to the abolition of slavery, to the creation of the Health Service. This is not just a matter of history. In the 1990s they led the Jubilee 2000 campaign for the remission of unpayable debt. They have been a voice for the voiceless and a witness for the very poorest in society. The Church of England alone covers every area of England through the parish system and is responsible for youth work, advice centres, and community groups wherever you look.

The Archbishops' Council of the Church of England, for example, continues to speak up for Christian charities and churches on matters of legislation which might require an exemption from the law. Even when defeated the Church continues to contribute. The Roman Catholic Church, which faced the greatest affront when its adoption agencies were closed under the Sexual Orientation Regulations, did not throw its "toys out of the pram" but continued to engage with the government and wider society. This is the nature of the Church in a democracy – not to be the dominant voice, but to earn the right to be heard through its experience, its witness, and the quality of its extensive thinking about the common good.

CHAPTER EIGHT

ESTABLISHMENT: A BULWARK AGAINST INTOLERANCE

The failure of historical memory must be one of the greatest contributors to Britain's modern apathy towards and unease with faith. In an increasingly consumerist, materialist world the pursuit of novelty has become the greatest gain.

In 1997, Tony Blair swept into power on the back of a wave of enthusiasm for change. His successful rebranding of the Labour Party emphasized its "newness", and a complete break with the past. This was accomplished ruthlessly from the top to the bottom of the Party; from the selection of candidates, to the abolition of that symbolic commitment to socialism, Clause 4. David Cameron has entered into a similar programme with regard to the Conservative Party in his attempt to remove the memory of Thatcherism and to break with the image of the "nasty party".

The way that both leaders communicated this branding was to emphasis the fact that Britain was being made "anew" rather than being "renewed". This is merely an illustration of recent attitudes towards the past. Traditions are regarded as boring, the past is often seen as wholly bad – a matter both of shame and indifference. We live in discomfort with our past – not least Britain's association with colonialism and empire. To add to this a confused curriculum has left us forgetful and confused.

It is hardly surprising therefore that despite the formal constitutional position of the Church of England, we find that our political leaders, the media, our educationalists, and public institutions do not behave as though there is an establishment where Christianity is central. Indeed, looking back I now realize that my eleven years as Archbishop of Canterbury was an interesting transitional time. It placed me very close to the monarchy and the government. I was often consulted in regular meetings with ministers on major matters of policy. Furthermore, at those times when I felt the Church's voice must necessarily be critical there was an open door to our political leaders. When it came to expressing the deepest moments of the nation's grief or celebration there was no uncertainty regarding the place where this should be focused – one of our national cathedrals, such as St Paul's.

Yet astonishingly, in the area of constitutional reform, the convention of consultation among Church and State and Crown has become contentious and neglected in recent years. To take one example, soon after he became prime minister, Gordon Brown waived his right to choose bishops – the custom by which two names are presented to him by the Crown Appointments Commission and he, representing the monarch, is able to choose either name or request others. This should not be construed as an attack on the then prime minister. In my opinion Gordon Brown served our country conscientiously and well. However, it is strange that neither the House of Bishops nor Synod saw that, at a stroke, a step had been taken by this son of the Kirk to loosen the ties of the Establishment with the minimum of consultation. Previous prime ministers took a healthy interest in the appointment of bishops. As James Callaghan observed, because twenty-six bishops sat in the House of Lords, the State had a legitimate interest.

The prime minister's decision to give up this role struck me as "cavalier" to say the least. Firstly, his duty came as a Royal Prerogative and therefore could not be said to be a mere preference for him to set aside. Both Church and Crown seem to have been bypassed. Although the Church of England was undoubtedly given very short notice of the change, the House of Bishops should not have accepted a major departure from a settled convention without a period of discussion. However well intended these constitutional decisions were, the problem lies in the fact that they can unbalance constitutional rights and duties.

We have seen other examples of this lack of joined-up thinking in other areas of constitutional reform. In 1998 the first step to House of Lords reform was undertaken with the abolition of the right of hereditary peers to sit in the House. This was an entirely correct first step, yet thirteen years later no further reform has been undertaken beyond that single act of constitutional surgery. Furthermore, other constitutional reforms have been piecemeal. The Privy Council Office has been all but abolished, as has the office of Lord Chancellor – one of the most ancient offices in the land. Furthermore, the Law Lords have been displaced from Parliament to a new Supreme Court. The danger of this scattergun approach to constitutional reform lies in the area of unintended consequences. Some, if not most, of these acts have been undertaken solely by prime ministerial fiat rather than as a consequence of a wide-ranging public debate. This approach harms the constitutional balance that has taken centuries to develop. It undermines respect for vital public institutions and creates uncertainty.

THE FACT OF ESTABLISHMENT

It is very probable that few know that the Church in this land is in some senses older than England itself. Certainly before there was a united England, there was a united English Church. Churchmen played an important role in the development of the idea of England, as counsellors and advisors to the Anglo-Saxon kings. Sometimes these churchmen would act as their critics, though some of my predecessors found it wise to offer their moral insights from the safety of northern France or Germany.

Despite the occasional falling-out, the Church and the king supported each other. And nowhere was this more clearly demonstrated than at the great coronation of King Edgar at Bath in ad 973. In a new and splendid ceremony, the king promised to fulfil the three duties of a Christian monarch: to protect God's Church; to punish malefactors; and to rule with justice and mercy. In return, the Archbishops of Canterbury and York anointed him, bestowing God's blessing and setting him above all other lords. That promise – or covenant – has remained central to royal coronations right up to modern times.

A strong sense of continuity flows in other channels too. It is sometimes forgotten, conveniently or otherwise, that our constitutional arrangements in the UK vest sovereignty in the monarch in Parliament under God. Not Parliament alone, but the monarch in Parliament, and both accountable to a higher, indeed a divine, moral authority.

But if this can be forgotten, or too easily disregarded, can it be said to really matter? Or is it a bit like the cross that perches on top of the clock tower housing Big Ben? It is there sure enough, but it is ornamental rather than instrumental. It has no bearing on whether the clock at Westminster strikes the hour or keeps good time.

My answer to the question "Does it matter?" is a simple and direct one: yes, it matters a great deal. I believe that it matters because so much else flows from it. It is through the sense of a higher, transcendent authority, to which we are all subject, that key concepts like service and duty, self-restraint and community, neighbourliness and solidarity, draw much of their sustaining strength and power. Without that sense, our human arrogance and selfishness, our inability to distinguish adequately between what is temporarily expedient and what serves the long-term common good, may all too easily get the better of us.

In England, the interweaving of Church and State and nation has come down to us through the long and steadily evolving set of relationships known as establishment – a partnership that has also taken various forms in other countries at different times. No one would argue that the process has been simple; few that it has been without flaws. But the fact is, of course, that we cannot abstract ourselves from the particularity of history.

Of course, establishment has evolved. One can only speculate as to how it may evolve in the future. What I am very clear about, however, is that no steps should be taken which would weaken the links between Church and State, without the very closest examination, both of their historic significance and of their wider impact on the community as a whole.

THE IMPORTANCE OF ESTABLISHMENT

This recent cavalier approach to the Church and State link is neglectful of a relationship that continues to matter. From the coronation of King Edgar at Bath in 973 to the wedding of Prince William and Kate Middleton at Westminster Abbey in April 2011, there is a seamless trajectory where Crown, Church, and State merge in a fruitful relationship.

Indeed, prior to that very wedding, I heard no voices putting forward alternative proposals for the wedding or rejecting the role of the Church. On the contrary, the reality it showed to the world is how important the role of the Christian faith remains to our nation. In this regard the Church of England has a primary responsibility to lead other churches in asserting the role of faith in the affairs of the nation. T. S. Eliot put the point rather well when he said "A people without religion will, in the end, find that it has nothing to live for." Ronald Reagan echoed that many years later: "Without God, there is no virtue, because there is no prompting of the conscience. Without God, we're mired in the material, that flat earth that tells us only what the senses perceive. Without God, there is a coarsening of society. And without God, democracy will not and cannot long endure."

We should not give in too quickly to the idea that we are living in a "secular" society. We have already noted the residual faith to which people say they belong when they respond to surveys or the national census. Why are we therefore now accepting that we are a post-Christian nation?

The huge majority of those who filled in that census question were declaring "We are not unbelievers: we identify ourselves with Christianity." This "declaration" gives the churches of this land permission and confidence to move among the people serving them and witnessing to them.

A SERVING ESTABLISHMENT

The role of the Church of England is indeed a peculiar one, originating in the medieval period when the Catholic Church, under the authority of the Pope, played a central role in the nation. At the Reformation, the church in England, breaking from the yoke of Rome, became the Church of England, in a special relationship with the sovereign and Parliament. By virtue of its establishment, the Church of England ministers to all in the land through its parish system, is governed nominally by the sovereign and Parliament, and has seats for bishops – the Lords Spiritual – in the House of Lords.

From the perspective of the Church of England, establishment helps to underwrite the commitment of a national Church to serve the entire community and to give form and substance to some of its deepest collective needs and aspirations. Part of the expression of that commitment may be so deep-rooted that it is taken utterly for granted as right and proper. At times of national celebration or mourning, for example, we expect great cathedrals to be a focal point of attention. That was true in the aftermath of the tragedies of 11 September 2001. It was also true when the Queen Mother passed away. At the regional level, Church of England bishops play major roles as community as well as spiritual leaders. But it is at the local level, perhaps, that the commitment that establishment underpins is most notable. The Church of England alone among religious groupings has a comprehensive network of parishes and priests covering the entire country: some 13,000 parishes in all, offering a ministry that is available to every member of the community. The strength and value of that undertaking was well demonstrated during the foot and mouth crisis of 2001 when local networks based round churches and parishes provided a vital lifeline to farming communities.

In urban and industrial communities too, the draining away of services and resources at periods of economic hardship has meant that the parish priest has been at times a crucial focus for keeping beleaguered neighbourhoods afloat and for breathing into them a vision of new life and worth and purpose. Sometimes the parish priest is the only professional person still living in the area that he or she serves.

As I have already observed, this "establishment" has evolved considerably over the centuries. At first, it had a vital role in "nation-building" and imposed a uniformity of liturgical practice. In 1689, the Toleration Act relaxed the expectations of uniformity for other Protestants, but Roman Catholics were only given equal freedom in the nineteenth century.

This has been a process of evolution, rather than revolution, creating an establishment that seeks to serve. For example, in the area of proposals for House of Lords reform, the bishops have always welcomed the prospect of the leaders of other churches and other faiths joining them to speak for faith more widely in the legislature. After the September 11 terrorist attacks in America in 2001, Prime Minister Tony Blair and I led an initiative to bring together Muslim and Christian leaders to reject violence and seek to build bridges.

The establishment of the Church of England is an impressive guarantor of religious freedom. The pre-eminence of Christianity does not disadvantage other faith groups, it actually gives them confidence that the voice of faith will be heard. This is a much more reassuring state of affairs for all believers, than a secularism which deems faith to be merely a matter of private opinion.

UNIQUE ROLE

But none of this does full justice to the fact that the Church – in which I include all the churches in Britain – has a deeper life and purpose. It is also the body of Christ, and at its heart is a set of spiritual values and beliefs that look beyond both time and place to eternity. The Church is here to draw people to the claims of Jesus Christ and to build the kingdom of God in the hearts and minds of men and women.

This is the point at which many, who are generally sympathetic to the Church and its role in society, tend to part company. They find it difficult to accept the claims of Christianity and are in some cases troubled and unsettled by those of us whose lives are shaped by it. From a Christian perspective, I am of course saddened by this, but I am also saddened by those people of faith who seem to think that it is only fellow believers who can really be inspired to build their life around ideas of service and selflessness, and around a sense of the inalienable dignity and worth of all humanity. The implication seems to be sometimes that others are just playing at it or doing it for some ulterior, self-serving motive.

This is not only wrong-headed; it misses a fundamental point. The values inherent in Christianity, and one needs to include here other faith traditions – including Judaism, to which Christians owe a great deal – are fundamental to the historical development of our culture and civilization, our concepts of justice and dignity, of service to others, and above all our understanding of the transforming power of love.

I have already mentioned the Church's role in education, which in England predates State provision. But a similar point can be made about many other aspects of society: about medicine and health care, about our legal system, about scientific research.

The reality is that Christianity has played a profound role in shaping the values and aspirations, institutions and forms of our society through the ages. I believe that it has been an overwhelmingly positive influence and remains crucial today for the sense of moral purpose and shared endeavour of the nation.

My concern is that without a sustaining belief in a source of moral authority lying beyond the individual's desires and ambitions, there is a real danger that important moral principles may be reduced to a matter of private opinion. Questions of right and wrong may become merely relative to what each person feels, so long as no actual harm is done to anyone else. I fear that the privatization of morality threatens to undermine our sense of cohesion, as society itself is broken down into a multiplicity of individual atoms; each doing its own thing with no commitment to agreed moral goals.

In today's world, of course, we shall not all agree about the precise source of authority which validates these values. But we need to understand that without the faith, hope and love that God plants in human hearts, without the commitment to living by a sturdy code of moral values, generation after generation, our collective prospects will be weakened. Without honesty, trust, faithfulness to an obligation, respect for the rights and interests of others and love of neighbour, civilized society falls apart.

A HOSPITABLE ESTABLISHMENT

The trajectory of the Church of England has been towards what I would call a "hospitable establishment". Hospitality requires a host. So, it is part of our role, I believe, to seek to provide space and access, opportunity and the right atmosphere for the many dealings and interactions between faith communities and the wider society, however and wherever we can. We seek to do this as a servant not as a master. There is nothing worse than a condescending host or an officious one who seeks to hog the limelight incessantly.

No one pretends that establishment does not involve challenges; no one doubts that it will continue to evolve and develop as it has always done. Equally, no one should pretend that the secular agenda to separate Church and State would not have far-reaching consequences. It is interesting that moving towards a secular basis for the State is something that many leaders of other faith communities strongly oppose. In his influential 1990 Reith Lectures, Jonathan Sacks, now Chief Rabbi, argued that "disestablishment would be a significant retreat from the notion that we share any values and belief at all… and a path to more, not fewer tensions".

He and others see in establishment and the historically rooted role of the Church of England an important protection against an unwanted and possibly unstable outcome. Those who dismiss establishment as the vestigial remains of religious privilege risk dishonouring not only the Church but also the concerns and aspirations of many other faith communities, whose rights they might claim to be championing.

This also provides a useful setting for the comment first made by the Prince of Wales in 1994 about understanding the role of the sovereign as "Defender of Faith". Without compromising in any way the centrality of Christianity and the Church of England to the spiritual life of the nation, it chimes well, I believe, with the concept of the "hospitable" establishment to which I referred earlier.

It also echoes the observation of that distinguished Anglican student of Islam, Bishop Kenneth Cragg, who has spoken of the way in which the concept of "hospitality" in relations between different faiths is linked crucially to the idea of "home". Put simply, in order to be hospitable to others, one first needs a home of one's own.

For we live in an increasingly rootless society. The patterns of our lives seem to become ever more provisional, improvised and at times, random. Of course, there is a sense in which mobility and novelty, chance and improvisation, can be both exciting and stimulating. The cult of the new clearly has some lasting appeal. I am certainly no enemy of change. And I have always seen honest doubt and a questioning spirit as two of faith's most stimulating friends.

But there is a sense in which we all need roots and security. Roots earth us in the rich soil of our shared history and traditions. Not, I believe, so that we are mired there, earth-bound and unable to move and develop, but so that we are able to draw strength and vitality for new growth and new flowering. Personal roots are important, but so are institutional ones – they are vital to the continuing organic growth and development of Church and society and to our sense of moral purpose and direction.

The unique role of the Church of England is therefore to seek to ensure the voice of faith is heard in the public domain. Our faith calls us to challenge decisions at both the national and the local level where the sidelining of faith is going on. I have said on more than one occasion that if we behave like a doormat we should not be surprised if we are treated as one. We must challenge unfairness in any form and stick up vigorously and strongly for the Christian faith. Sometimes we Christians are too polite, too nice, too reasonable, too obedient for our own good. I have noticed over the years that when groups take to the streets and complain to the media, politicians take notice and pay attention to what is going on. Muslims are particularly politically aware and take to the streets to complain where they feel their faith and their communities have been insulted or ignored. There may be times when we shall need to protest and witness publicly our concerns, our determination not to be regarded as doormats.

Those of us who have leadership in any way in church life should pay much more attention to the political nature of the gospel we believe in. Christ calls us to engage with life and that means entering into the needs of the world. Is the teaching we are getting in our churches too pietistic, too withdrawn from daily life? Are we focusing too much on individual faith and not sufficiently enough on living as Christians in the world?

CHAPTER 9

CHALLENGING THE CULTURE

The Church cannot accept as its role simply the winning of individuals to a kind of Christian discipleship which concerns only the private and domestic aspects of life. To be faithful to a message which concerns the kingdom of God, his rule over all things and all peoples, the church has to claim the high ground of public truth.[54]

These words of that late, great, missionary bishop, Lesslie Newbigin when he published his authoritative work, *The Gospel in a Pluralist Society* should continue to inspire the outward-looking Church today. Newbigin's contention was that while the Church can accept plurality, it cannot accept pluralism. By pluralism, he meant a society in which all truth was relative and subjective. The belief there were no absolute rights, wrongs, and norm would be a disaster

54 Lesslie Newbigin, *The Gospel in a Pluralist Society*, London: SPCK, 1989.

145

to society at large, he considered. He also pointed out that "secularization" – the aim of privileging no religion, in order to safeguard all of them – hid a further expectation: the disappearance of religious belief altogether.

Such beliefs are myths, he claimed. The secular society we inhabit is in fact a pagan society worshipping false gods. The solution he counselled lay not in seeking a return to Christendom when Christianity was imposed with the force of law, because that was itself a betrayal of the gospel. Nor could it be found in a secularism in which Christianity is one option among many because that inevitably limited faith to the private sphere. In fact a new kind of enlightenment was needed: "namely the opening up of the underlying assumptions of a secular society, the asking of the unasked questions, the probing of unrecognized presuppositions".

Newbigin's call was for a "confident" apologetic by Christians to challenge our culture. In our sights should be the privatization of belief and morality, the secularism which we sadly accepted, the pluralism which has relativized the truth, and the equality/rights culture which has distorted the image of humanity.

SECULARISM

Firstly let us take a look at secularism. Max Weber's theory of secularization suggested that rationalization, industrialization, and bureaucratization led to a society without religion. He and many other sociologists viewed this as an irreversible path in many ways to be welcomed amid European memories of horrific wars of religion, in which whole societies were torn to pieces purportedly over differences in doctrine. One aspect of "secularization" that has gripped the imagination most deeply is the onward progress of the forces of enlightenment that would inevitably displace religious belief with rationality.

It is amazing how deeply this general theory of secularization has permeated our culture. So many among our elites still believe one variety of this theory or other, despite the fact that religious belief is as strong as it ever was and shows no sign of dying. This is perhaps the fundamental reason for the rage felt by the most militant secularists: that all their theories about the waning of religion have been tested in the real world, and found to be wanting.

Nevertheless, we should not deny or avoid the fact that significant shifts have happened to our society in the last sixty years that has sidelined the Christian faith. There is much debate over how this happened and what are the constituent elements of the trend. Certainly, increased leisure opportunities have played their part, as has been the revolution in travel. The world has opened up so amazingly that the church that was central to community a hundred years ago has been thrust aside. This came home to me when I became vicar of St Nicholas's Durham in 1975. I happened to light upon the diary of the church for 1925, and found that the Sunday school numbered over 1,000, and when the Sunday school had its summer outing to places like Seaburn or Barnard Castle, the church was forced to hire a train. In 1975 the Sunday school numbered less than twenty.

What are the features of the present spiritual landscape? One notable element is the widely accepted distinction between being "religious" and being "spiritual". I am not at all sure when this division occurred. It is not uncommon to hear people say, "I am a spiritual person. I don't need religion to feed my inner soul. Religion is all about rules and authority. Spirituality is about feelings, about searching for truth, and finding authenticity in being."

It does no good to criticize the inadequacies of such personal spiritualities. We can point to their subjectivism and rejection of community. We can object that their rejection of religion is unfair and un-factual. But what is undeniable is that many people feel that they are no longer comfortable with being described as "religious".

So, one feature of our spiritual landscape is that with a decline in the numbers of those who profess a faith in an orthodox denomination, there are a growing number whose spirituality is anchored to a bewildering number of positions. Some are those who have simply fallen away from practising Anglicanism, Catholicism, or Methodism, but still regard themselves as such. Others are bolder in practising a faith but their beliefs are not compatible with that of the mother church to which they claim to belong. For example, Tony and Cherie Blair have clearly publicly stated that they ignored the Catholic Church's teaching on contraception, and the Catholic Church, remarkably, has not criticized their stance.

We cannot turn the clock back. The Church, in all its forms, faces a daunting challenge to engage with a society and culture that, in spite of its unambiguous Christian inheritance, is now diverse and complex. However, what is very interesting is that comparatively few people have rejected Christianity or religion generally on intellectual grounds. Those who are secular for intellectual reasons are very small in number. In the words of Grace Davie, committed secularism "remains the creed of a relatively small minority".

Indeed, the idea of the secular society faces its most severe challenge, not from vitality of religious belief, but from the dearth of rationality. The Catholic commentator Damian Thompson claims that we are facing a "pandemic of credulous thinking". Even otherwise intelligent people often accept "counter knowledge" – ideas which are fiction masquerading as fact – including conspiracy theories of various kinds. The plethora of new superstitions and wacky ideas appears to have grown in a period in which institutional faith is dying. This phenomenon gives the lie to the idea that religion is replaced with rationality.

Without labouring the point, it also needs to be pointed out that the completely "secular" state very often does not do away with the wars of religion, rather it conducts its own wars against religion or other competing ideas. Consider the millions killed under Stalin and the persecution of religious believers in the eastern European bloc, China, and Korea. Chairman Mao supervised the mass murder of more people than Stalin and Hitler put together. Those who glibly state that "religion has done more harm than good" are silenced by the fact that Stalin, Hitler, Mao, and Pol Pot were secular leaders.

The claim that the secularism is an irreversible process has certainly some credibility. All the signs point in that direction. Charles Taylor in his landmark book *A Secular Age* comments on the "retreat of Christendom": "It will be less and less common for people to be drawn into or kept within a faith by some strong political or group identity, or by the sense that they are sustaining a socially essential ethic."[55] Of course, this has been happening in Britain for a very long time. However, Taylor does not see this retreat

55 Charles Taylor, *A Secular Age*, Belknap Press of Harvard University Press, 2007, p. 514.

as indicating the death of faith. He argues, as I will shortly, that secularism does not have sufficient inner strength or meaning to sustain unbelief. Human aspiration to faith will not flag. And neither will secularism ever be a beacon of progress and enlightenment.

Nevertheless, the idea of secularism has its uses: it helps towards a separation of Church and State, which rules out the kind of uniformity of belief which has often been imposed during the course of European history. Christian societies have often upheld this separation of powers before any others and this is because the idea of such a separation is intrinsic to Christianity. This, of course, is the opposite of Islam where, from the beginning, Muslim communities have prioritized sharia law over civic or secular law. Many Muslims will agree that this constitutes Islam's greatest argument with the West and is its Achilles heel. The Christian position stems from the story in the Gospels where Christ held up a Roman coin in answer to hostile questioners who are trying to trap Jesus into opposing the Roman authorities and said "Give back to Caesar what is Caesar's, and to God what is God's" (Matthew 22:21). This has been seen as a way of sidestepping the question – which of course, it wasn't – but it has also been foundational to Christian political thought. St Paul also insists in Romans 13 that Christians are obliged to obey earthly authorities.

We should note that this does not suggest a slavish

devotion to the State but rather a robust relationship. Indeed, although both Christ and Paul did challenge earthly authorities, these strands of early Christian theology seem to establish some degree of separation which was later to be reversed when Christianity became identified with earthly power after Constantine's conversion. This lay the foundation of an era often referred to as "Christendom" when the Church compelled and coerced belief (or at least lip service to belief) through the use of law and the exercise of temporal power. Regrettably, religious conflicts over doctrine did indeed become the presenting cause of persecutions, wars, and massacres.

Bringing this up to date, Christians have always been on unsure ground when they have sided with secular authorities. Christians have sometimes been in the wrong place on such matters, in terms of criminalizing behaviour with which they disagree. The blasphemy law which imposed criminal penalties was often defended even very recently by the Church of England despite the fact that it was effectively defunct. It was pointed to as a symbol of the Church–State link. If so, it was completely the wrong symbol. It represented faith as a coercive power and the Church as a tyrant. Christianity's strength lies in its gentle power of persuasion and the Church's call to "servanthood".

HUMAN RIGHTS

Another area in which our culture has taken a wrong term and in which fundamental misconceptions need to be questioned is in the area of equality and human rights – a battleground that dominates the theme of this book. It was in the Middle Ages when the concept of "rights" was first brought together within the combined Roman law concepts, *dominium* (ownership) and *ius* (justice). This was effectively an "ownership" of a particular aspect of justice – a right being "moral property". This concept of "rights" flourished in the seventeenth and eighteenth centuries with the English Bill of Rights (1689), the Bill of Rights of Virginia (1776) and the French Declaration of the Rights of Man and the Citizen (1789). It was after the Second World War that the international human rights movement could be said to have come into being.

In recent discourse, legal and moral rights are distinctively recognized. According to Julian Rivers,[56] a legal right "formally recognizes an element of justice as it applies to an individual and empowers that individual to achieve justice through a legal system". In contrast, a moral right "is a justified power that one person has over another because of who they are". Legal rights are granted while moral rights are inherent. It is not necessary to accept the existence of

---

56 *Christianity in a Changing World: Beyond the Morality of Rights*, London: Marshall Pickering, 2000.

153

moral rights even if you accept the need for legal rights.

In an excellent discussion of rights, Rivers concludes that there is in reality no language of "rights" in the Bible. The closest the Old Testament comes to the concept is *mishpat*, referring to the practical aspects of justice. While the word "right" can be used in modern translations of the New Testament, this tends to refer to "power", "authority". Paul uses the term *exousia* extensively in 1 Corinthians in the context of "rights" or "authority" which are renounced in favour of the way of love. Similarly, Jesus taught that his followers must be prepared to give up their "rights" to follow the way of the cross.

"The Christian then, can accept the existence of rights, but must move beyond rights to consider how they should be exercised," writes Rivers, "Living the Christ-like, virtuous life involves reflection on how I can make best use of my 'normative property' in the knowledge that I am accountable to God for that use."[57]

Rights language often goes hand in hand with the idea of autonomy and certain rights therefore accrue to us because we have a "right" to be in control of our own lives and outcomes. Other rights are, of course, dependent on the rights of another.

Much discussed in recent years is dichotomy of "rights" vs "responsibilities", though it would probably be truer in Christian terms to think of these in terms of "rights" vs

57 Ibid.

154

"virtues". Yet the fact is that for the Christian to talk about rights, is more often to talk about the sacrifice of those rights in favour of others. In the most practical example of this, we have Christ giving up his "right to life" for the sake of us all. This must lead us to question whether Christians should in any circumstances seek to challenge for their "rights" in the courts over and against the "rights" of other minorities. This is at the heart of many of the cases we have highlighted in earlier chapters. Yet while the Christian may decide to put those rights aside, we cannot really ask anyone to act against their conscience, nor can we expect them to forego their rights in the knowledge that others may suffer if they do not take a stand. Yet we must beware entering into the cultural conflicts through the courts with a purely autonomous view of our own "rights". The imagery of the "community" in the Bible, through the rich imagery of *koinonia*, the interrelationship of the Trinity, and the theme of interdependent parts of the body must lead us to oppose the view that "rights" are autonomous, any more than the individual is autonomous.

There is yet another fundamental conflict between the language of "rights" and the Christian faith and it is here that the category of "equality" comes into the equation. At the heart of Christian teaching is the notion that we are all God's children. In the new covenant there are no "Jews or Greeks", "rich or poor", "male or female", "slave or free".

To this list could be added "black or white" and "straight or gay". There is absolute equality between us because we are all made in the image of our loving heavenly father. Yet we are also absolutely morally corrupt and in need of God's loving grace. In modernity, we are equal because we are all equally esteemed. In Christian terms, we are equally in need of redemption. Thus at the heart of the modern notion of equality is a fundamental relativism. There is no distinction between "being" and "doing". The "rights" of the adulterer are equal to the rights of the forsaken spouse – there can be no distinction, no "judgment" between them. And it is primarily here that the Christian has his deepest disagreement with prevalent ideas because "rights", if based only on issues of equality, have abandoned a moral position anchored on justice.

We can see now that the Christian world view is startlingly different from a secular viewpoint. One has a clear base in a transcendent God from whom all moral life and meaning flows. The other finds no such basis for belief and positions itself on the absence of God and man as the measure of all things.

However, it is my contention that Christian people have nothing to fear from the situation we are in. To some degree Western Christians have had it far too easy; we have not known persecution for hundreds of years and for that time we have occupied centre ground. If we are being challenged, then that can only lead to a fresh "reformation" of life and to what I call a post-secular existence, because it is my firm view that humanism is ultimately barren.

THE FUTURE OF CHRISTIANITY IN A SECULAR EUROPE

Throughout this short book we have been examining the extraordinary changes that have happened in Britain and Europe in the space of a few years. Our current situation raises momentous questions about the nature of the Church as well as the styles of ministry, evangelism, and service it should employ to stay relevant to the needs of our time.

Some will immediately pounce on this word "relevant". Surely, they will say, " God does not require us to be relevant but faithful." They might even go on to quote that well-known saying of Dean William Inge: "A church that marries the spirit of the age becomes the widow of the next generation." That warning should not be an excuse for doing nothing. The Church has always changed and has always adapted in different ways to society around us. Relevance is a key principle for Christian mission and need not be in competition with faithfulness to it.

No one has explored this more helpfully than Richard Niebuhr in his 1951 book, *Christ and Culture*. Niebuhr considered that relationships between the Christian community and secular society constituted an "enduring problem" that had been treated in different ways down the centuries but, in modern times, had become a matter for urgent concern as the distance between secularism and faith widened. The book is too rich and complex to be easily simplified, but in five models he traces the way the Christian faith and culture may clash, coexist or diverge.

The first – and most radical – Christ Against Culture, assumes that the relationship between the Church and culture is that of light and darkness. Niebuhr cites as examples the third-century church father, Tertullian, Tolstoy the Russian writer, and the Mennonites. Tolstoy consistently argued that "All state obligations are against the conscience of a Christian – the oath of allegiance, taxes, law proceedings and military service." Without going as far as that, there are many examples in contemporary Christianity of churches that take an uncompromising attitude in rejecting the world. I have had experience of that when my Christian life began as a teenager. My church in Dagenham, to which I owe more than I can possibly say, taught the young people that society around was a place of darkness. Citing passages like 1 John 2:15 ("Do not love the world or anything in the world") and 2 Corinthians 6:17 ("come out from them and be separate"), we were told never to go to the theatre, cinema, pubs, and similar places. It took me some years to see that, although there are certain truths within the warnings, this overall rejection of culture sat very uneasily with following the Jesus who mixed freely with sinners and ate with them.

Niebuhr's second model is that of the Christ of Culture. In history, he noted, there were those who claimed that Christ is to be understood as the highest aspiration and fulfilment of culture. This approach inevitably leads to accommodation – the attempt to reconcile Christianity with society around. Niebuhr cited Enlightenment thinkers Locke, Kant, and Jefferson who, in different ways, tried to isolate a form of Christian faith to show that it was entirely compatible with culture around. It is unnecessary for me to point to such attempts today where previously rejected ethical positions are now accepted as the norm. In *The Screwtape Letters*, C. S. Lewis spoke of attempts in his day of cultural movements being endorsed by what he called "Christianity and...": Christianity and Communism; Christianity and Psychic Research; Christianity and Vegetarianism.

A third option for Niebuhr was Christ Above Culture. According to this model, neither rejection nor a blank affirmation of culture was required but a synthesis of the two. According to Niebuhr, Thomas Aquinas is considered a good example of this model because he held that the Church must promote humankind's temporal goals as well as leading it beyond the world. There is much that is good in this picture also. The model attempts a fine balance between seeing Christ as part of culture (born in a specific culture) and yet outside culture (as sustaining it and leading beyond it). However, as Niebuhr points out, by synthesizing Christianity with culture this approach may lead to the institutionalizing of Christ and the gospel. This option tends to treat culture as being neutral – neither good nor bad. This is sadly not so. Societies may become very bad indeed – think of Nazi Germany and other examples closer to home – and identification with them may lead to the corruption of the faith itself.

Seeing that the synthesist option has weaknesses, Niebuhr then introduces another model – that of Christ and Culture in Paradox. He states that there have been those in history whose approach to Christianity and the world has been "both-and". St Augustine stands out, as does Martin Luther, with his "two kingdoms" theology. Richard Niebuhr offers the view that supporters of this model see an overlap and a tension between the two authorities. This tension he describes as a "paradox", because both sin and grace mix in human experience and in the world. Luther, for example, taught that Christians who are under the banner of Christ "need no temporal law or sword" because good works naturally flow from grace. He stated "a good tree needs no instruction how to bear good fruit". On the other hand, in his horror at the Peasants' Revolt, Luther was an outspoken advocate of temporal justice: in his view, laws were there to be obeyed.

What do we make of this approach to the world around

us? As Richard Niebuhr saw it, there were strengths and weaknesses. The strength of the position is that it takes seriously the fact of sin and grace in life and in human institutions. Sin exists even in the most Christian of institutions through which, paradoxically, the work of Christ may continue its cleansing activity in the world around. But, charges Niebuhr, the most serious weakness is that it can lead to a cultural conservatism because the instinct is to see the two "worlds" existing side by side with sin and grace penetrating both. The result is often to let state and economic life alone, and allow it to continue unchanged. Christians focus more on the area of the religious, or church life, leaving social affairs in the world to be attended by others. I have to say, from my experience growing up in Dagenham that this seemed to be the theology of my church. The vicar's entire attention was on leading people to the Lord – which he did effectively – but I do not recall a sermon that related the faith to the outside world. There are still many churches that are strongly dualist in nature.

Niebuhr's final model is entitled Christ: The Transformer of Culture. Without saying as much, Niebuhr implies that this model comes closest to what he actually believes: it is a "conversionist" approach to culture which belongs to the "great central tradition of the church". What distinguishes conversionists from the previous group is their more positive attitude towards culture – that God is at work still in creation and human life and that much of human activity is good and wholesome. This option still affirms the universality of sin, but maintains that culture can be reformed, changed, and converted.

Unlike the other models, Niebuhr does not offer criticisms of the conversionist model but it too has strengths and weaknesses. The positive features are in its view that we can work in society for its betterment because God is at work in the world and we can cooperate with the Holy Spirit in creation. Many examples spring to mind: that of William Wilberforce in Parliament to name but one.

If Niebuhr considered that this "enduring problem" was relevant for the period immediately after the last world war where issues of secularism were beginning to emerge strongly, most observers will agree that the twenty-first century is now experiencing the problem at gale force strength. Forces are now blowing in Western society to silence the voice of faith and privatize its work. The Church is being driven from the world and individuals victimized if they dare challenge the norms of society. And this problem is not only being felt in the UK. In his ground-breaking book, *The Culture of Disbelief*, Stephen L. Carter, a professor of law in the USA, recounts the story of a Colorado public school teacher who "was ordered by his superiors, on pain of disciplinary action, to remove his personal Bible from his desk where students might see it".[58] Such cases in the States, as in the UK, are typical, as we have seen, of a trend towards what Richard John Neuhaus called "the naked public square" in which public discourse and institutions are deprived of all associations with religion. Carter's diagnosis is that the religious views of the vast majority of Americans are being reduced to the level of a hobby "like building model airplanes – something quiet, something private, something trivial".

I fully recognize that some Christians are content to be left alone and Niebuhr's examination offers some clues as to why some prefer it that way. But if we take Christianity at all seriously, the privatization of this religion is at odds with a genuine Christian vocation which, of necessity, involves a visible expression of faith. Theologian Helmut Thielicke said memorably "Woe unto you, if you, the servant of God, do not tell the State what it is and what it owes to God... If you really give God what belongs to him, then that will not occur in your hymn singing and church services... You must bear your message into public life; you must be the salt of the earth."[59]

Of course, being the salt of the earth, or lights to the world – which was the other great image that Jesus used of his followers in society – is never easy. But, by the same token, neither is it very hard in our country. I trust that in my

---

58 Stephen L. Carter, *The Culture of Disbelief*, Anchor, 1994, p. 11.
59 *Being Human, Becoming Human*, Garden City, Lincoln, University of Nebraska, 1984, p. 256.

lifetime as a man from a working-class culture, serving in Her Majesty's Forces, and earning my living in the world, I have never backed away from declaring my faith, courteously yet firmly, to others. Yes, I have experienced contempt and some opposition on the way, as a layman and as a clergyman, but I have never experienced persecution or direct opposition and discrimination that some Christians abroad in other cultures have encountered. This, of course, may change as time goes on, but if Christianity is more than a hobby, then it must take us into areas of confrontation from time to time.

WHAT THEN ARE THE IMPLICATIONS FOR THE CHRISTIAN FAITH TODAY?

In my opinion never have we had a better moment to see the Christian life as the most amazing adventure with the God who calls us to follow. We have all inherited static versions of the Church – the Church as the "body of Christ", the "people of God" – but very few have been conscious of the Church as a pioneering body that pushes out into the world in service and mission. Lesslie Newbigin, the great missiologist who died in 1998, once observed that there was a great desire among the clergy in the UK to minimize the distinction between the Church and the world and instead to emphasize the goodness of the world as God's creation.

The result, he said, was to affirm the continuity between the good things of human culture and the perfection of them by grace in the life of the Church. How clearly this mirrors Niebuhr's models. Of course, Newbigin, who appreciated human culture, was not denying that there is continuity, but his observation was that the blurring of the difference led to the softening of mission and little difference between the Church and the world. He offers a powerful image of the relationship between Church and culture in terms of a paradigm shift between two realities. To Saul the Pharisee, Jesus and his followers could only be seen as an enemy, a subverter of the law, and therefore had to be challenged. But to Paul, the Christian, the same law now reinterpreted, could be seen as a guardian to lead him to Christ. The old paradigm – two faiths in collision – cannot make sense of the new, but the new can make sense of the old. Most of us can testify to this interpretation. As we look back we can see that there was much in our formation and culture that led us to faith in Christ, but there were aspects we had to reject, which were not compatible with the new life we are called to live.

And it has everything to do with whether mission is central to our lives and at the heart of the Christian churches. I recall some years ago attending a fashionable event in London. Over cocktails, an eminent man approached me with champagne in his hands and said: "Archbishop, I used to be a practising Christian but I have fallen by the wayside.

Do you know why?" Seeing my questioning look he went on: "Because I realized that there was a real discrepancy between what Christians believed and what they practised. If they truly believed that a personal relationship with Jesus Christ has serious implications for eternity, there are too few Christians who seem to believe it and even fewer who put it into practice."

Sadly he was right. The passion is lacking. The demanding commitment of being a follower of Jesus Christ, blazing new trails of service and leaving everything to journey into the unknown is not the norm, if it ever was. To be sure, there are plenty of Christian people who are committed to their churches and who work faithfully to keep worship going and the building in good order – and we are grateful to them. But that is not mission. Worship is not the engine room of Christianity, mission is. When worship is decoupled from the burning heart of evangelism our distinctiveness is lost and our focus is blurred. From my experience of over fifty years in Christian service I have to say that churches that have mission at the heart of their existence are pitifully few and those who have, are not only from the evangelical tradition.

I still remember visiting Fr Paul Diamond's church in Bermondsey years ago for an anniversary and finding to my joy and amazement a form of mission that brought together all the strands of the Church in a harmonious whole. Paul Diamond, who sadly died in his prime, had such a love of God, united with a love of people, and a genuine sense of mission that people were drawn into a loving Christian family. Fr Paul was in every sense a committed Anglo-Catholic but he fused the traditions together in such a natural way that the old divisions did not seem to matter. There have been other examples of the same genuine sense of mission in the evangelical tradition also, and such churches are able to reach out into their communities in a strong and affirming manner. But too many others do not and one senses that mission is rather an afterthought, tagged on hopefully rather than a thought out and conscious desire to make disciples.

The implication of the approach I am suggesting does not imply a hostile rejection of the culture around us, but a recognition of much goodness within it, as well as a critical awareness of its deficiencies. A faith that has at its heart the coming of the Lord into human society cannot have a wholly negative view of human life. Christians believe that every human person is made in the image of God and this is the launch pad for mission and service. In other words, authentic Christianity means engagement with our societies, not defensively, but with confidence and with hope. Quite frankly, the best examples in my experience come not from our Britain but from my visits to other countries. I think, for example, of the Anglican diocese of Egypt where Mouneer Anis is the current bishop. Mouneer was at one time the senior physician of Harper Memorial Hospital, Menif, until his sudden appointment as bishop of the diocese in 2000. The diocese is small, some 25,000 souls or thereabouts, but there is no gainsaying its effective ministry. And that is the interesting thing, because the ministry of the diocese of Egypt is much wider and richer than most dioceses in the Church of England. There is considerable input into health, education, deaf schools, special schools, as well as theological education. The diocese is quite poor and reliant on the West but the focus of putting resources where the Church is working is very effectively done. There is a seamless unity between mission – reaching out in the widest sense through humanitarian concern – and evangelism – preaching the gospel and leading others to Christ. In a country where direct evangelism is forbidden, the diocese has to pick its way carefully through an Islamic culture where Christian activity is regarded suspiciously. Mouneer has good relationships with the Grand Imam and Grand Mufti and is bold in his witness to them.

In spite of the restrictions, the Church is growing and converts are being made. There is a quiet optimism and much to encourage this small and effective church. I could say similar things about other parts of the Anglican Communion where minority churches put us to shame by their enthusiasm, love, and deep desire to bring the love of God to others.

Years ago, when I was a teacher on the staff of St John's

Nottingham I was on the top deck of a bus with my daughter Rachel. The bus stopped outside Christ Church, Chilwell. Rachel, then ten years or so, looking at people coming out of the church said: "Daddy, what are churches for?" I cannot recall what I said, but her question has haunted me ever since. It has been my privilege to visit many churches since I became a bishop in 1987 and what has struck me has been the need to be liberated to think more holistically. Our task is to be more adventurous in turning our churches into vibrant communities that are more authentic expressions of the kingdom of God, than we have at present.

How may we do that? Let me make some suggestions in the light of our present challenges.

1. To be real communities of Jesus Christ

There is no such thing as a church where Jesus is absent. But giving him centrality and priority should be our most important task. It means being committed to him, in the church, and deepening the prayer life and worship of the people of God. The church is only bearable to the extent that Christ is visible within it. The Romanian pastor, Petru Dumitriu, expressed this well in his own struggles with his church:

It is impossible to be a Christian.
It is impossible not to be a Christian.
It is impossible to be a Christian within the Church.
And the Church is impossible.[60]

60 Petru Dumitriu, *To the Unknown God*, trans. James Kirkup, Collins, 1982.

We all have some sympathy with that cry, but when a congregation is gathered around the Lord, and united in witness, so the church becomes a servant of the gospel and not master of it.

2. We must become communities of action

From the beginning of the Christian era, faith and action have never been separated. To those who believe that the Christian faith has made no material difference to this world, we have only to point to the clear evidence that in practically every area of social care from health to education, from medicine to agriculture, from dentistry to water aid, Christians have made major contributions. There can be no challenge to these facts. The gospel is never other-worldly but practical and caring. If the gospel is not taking practical form in our churches, we are depriving the world of its power.

3. We must become communities of forgiveness and acceptance

Sadly, too many churches are places where ordinary people are uncomfortable because the impression that outsiders gather is that the church does not welcome sinners. There is a great need for Christian communities to be places of genuine welcome, where relationships of trust are made and where friendship is key.

4. We must become communities of fun and celebration

There is too little fun and joy in church life at present and yet, curiously, that is how Jesus described the kingdom – as a place where there is much celebration, joy, and laughter. Even though being a Christian is serious business, is there not a place for joy in our churches?

5. We need to become communities that transcend the gulf between the ages and where the elderly as much as the young are welcomed

Sadly, in many churches in the UK, young people are missing and there should be a concerted effort to bring children and teenagers back into the worshipping community. This requires serious investment of time and money, and bishops and church leaders must ensure that every church makes this a priority.

6. We should advertise more confidently the advantages of being a Christian today

In all our neighbourhoods, the service of Christian communities and their witness in social and ethical matters is extraordinarily impressive. As Roy Hattersley has pointed out, church people are likely to be more committed to serving others than most non-churchgoers; they give to charities more than non-churchgoers; they are often to be found abroad serving the very poor of the world, than most non-churchgoers. In a 2011 survey of Evangelical Alliance members,[61] 25 per cent of those surveyed were found to be trustees of a registered charity (compare that to 2.2 per cent nationally). Nine per cent serve as school governors (compared to 0.7 per cent nationally) and 4 per cent are members of a political party (compared to 1.3 per cent nationally). They are also more likely to serve as councillors and magistrates and an astonishing 91 per cent of them turned out to vote in the AV referendum in May 2011. The contribution of Christians to society is often remarkable.

We can take this further. Church attendance improves health! Studies on both sides of the Atlantic have shown that this is the case. The Graduate School of Public Health at Pittsburgh University has established a Consortium on Faith and Health which concluded a study with the words: "People who regularly attend religious services have been found to have lower blood pressure, less heart disease, lower rates of depression and generally better health than those who don't attend."[62] When we move from personal health to the health of societies, a similar argument may be mounted. Young people who are in church communities or church programmes are less sexually promiscuous, less involved in drug activities, engage in less binge drinking, less likely to be truant from school, and are involved in less crime. This

---

61 http://www.eauk.org/snapshot/upload/Does-Belief-touch-society.pdf
62 Carnegie Samuel Calian, *Survival or Revival: Ten Keys to Church Vitality*, Westminster John Knox Press, 1999, p. 79.

does not make them "goody-goodies", indeed they remain ordinary happy teenagers, but their lifestyles are healthier and their life-prospects more promising.

SALT AND LIGHT

I have always been struck by Jesus' emphasis on his followers being "salt" and "light" in society. By saying this he was not outlining this as an option for us in a future pure community, but in the here and now. We are expected to make a difference. The parable of Jesus concerning leaven or yeast picks up the same refrain, that the presence of Jesus in the world – through his followers – can and should change society. We have something important to add and the values enshrined in the Christian faith can influence secular society. There is a challenge here for ministers in their task of helping congregations "discriminate" between what is good and wholesome, and what is not.

But being "salt, light and leaven" also relates to our engagement with the world around us. Why was William Wilberforce so vexed about slavery? The issue did not concern him directly, and he could have enjoyed a comfortable and successful political life without being bothered by a problem that affected people outside the UK. His engagement with it came from two main sources: first from a conscience shaped and enlightened by his faith and, second, by his responsibilities as a politician. He was not afraid to take his faith into parliamentary debates and face considerable opposition. The same can be said of many other reformers of whom the churches should be very proud.

Is there not a need for ministers to help their congregations not only discriminate in matters to do with morals and personal ethics but also in shaping the world around us? In many respects this is already happening. In more than a few places, local charities would collapse were Christians not involved. I think we can do more. A relevant faith is one that reaches out and is alert to the changing needs of our world.

I am writing this after the riots in Tottenham in the summer of 2011, riots that alarmingly spread quickly to other parts of England. Within a few hours, a protest of moral indignation at the shooting by police of a young man became an opportunistic plundering of shops and businesses, looting, burning, and destroying. CCTV footage picked up pictures of people being robbed. A terrified woman leapt from a burning building. Three men who had been protecting their property were deliberately run down.

A number of commentators have already linked this collapse of order to the decline of moral values in our society. Other explanations have pointed to fatherlessness and the failure of parental responsibility together with poverty and a lack of education. Yet the context to these riots has been the general collapse of public trust in our institutions. In recent years we have witnessed the failure of the banks, scandals in Parliament, the press, and the police. Many people are increasingly coming round to the view that society itself has lost its way with no sure anchor in strong moral foundations.

The churches must also share the blame. Consumerism, an idol of the modern world, is a powerful factor in the lives of many Christians. A gospel of prosperity is present as never before. In the wake of the riots, some Christian commentators have asked whether our churches have been sufficiently robust in challenging a culture of greed. The challenge is a fair one. I don't think we have stood out as well as we should have done in combating a false religion in which possessions, income, and affluence have become the sole hallmarks of success. It is time to speak up for lifestyles that focus on being rather than having; on quality of life rather than quantity of things.

Unless our faith takes a "political" form it runs the risk of being divorced from our communities. I am not talking about party politics, for Christians are represented in all of them, but rather community life and decision-making. They are engaged in society but at the civic level in the life of churches and parishes their contribution is often out of sight. I am dismayed that so few churches are engaged in outreach and action and are known not to be interested. I know it from reading parish and church magazines that indicate little connection between the church and local society. I know it from discussions with clergy who tell me that they are not dealing with issues like poverty, the elderly, and the young. It doesn't take a lot to make connections, to show interest and to take up one or two platforms that emanate from the Christian faith itself.

We live in testing yet thrilling times for Christian believers. All churches can demonstrate that following in the steps of the young leader, Jesus, leads to a rewarding present, and a glorious future: a hope that nothing else can match. The recovery of our apostolate is essential to the Church's mission and future. Just as at the start of Christianity, the Church of the third Millennium has a wonderful opportunity to proclaim afresh the life-changing gospel of Jesus Christ to our world. If we can regain our sense of being God's instrument for transformation we may well set the world ablaze once more. On that decision hinges the future of the Church in England.